The Book of Sprague

A casual history and look at all-things Sprague as found throughout the Internet

Compiled by Jeffrey Sprague

Copyright 2015 by Jeffrey Sprague

All Rights Reserved

No original part of this book, or the aggregation, may be reproduced without written permission from the author or his agents.

Welcome to the family.

1st *Printing – December 2015*

Table of Contents

About the Information in this Collection

This is not, by any stretch of the imagination, a thoroughly-vetted, academically worthy piece of research. This book contains two basic types of information:

- Examples of my own ancestral line, to which the majority of Spragues will eventually intersect.
- Pretty much anything and everything I could find on the internet about "Spragues" – people, places, and things, slightly edited and formatted for this book.

I claim a copyright on my work of aggregating these sources together and formatting them for this book, so I ask you not to copy it. Countless evenings and scores of precious hours were put into collecting, editing, and formatting this. I do not claim authorship, ownership, or copyright on most of the individual pieces of content contained within. Much of the information came from Wikipedia, Google Maps, FamilySearch.org, Ancestry.com. Except for my own timeline and family data, almost everything in this book can be found on-line on public sites. This book simply collects it together for your convenience. I believe I am not violating (at least not seriously) any copyrights by aggregating this publically available and publically posted reference material into a convenient form that is intended for non-profit educational or instructional purposes. Hopefully you will find some valuable nuggets of information, or simply the inspiration to jump into your own family history.

Introduction

One of the most mind-blowing thought-games I've ever contemplated deals with ancestry. The next time you are feeling unlucky, consider this: your ancestral line has survived *every single* mutation and generation all the way back to the original amoeba swimming in that first puddle of swamp goo. Not once, at any point in these millions and millions of iterations did a single one of your ancestors die before successfully spawning the next generation. Mind blown.

Now, of course, when you trace any series of events backwards in time, the odds of the results are 100% because it's already happened and the result is known, but think about the odds of that first primitive cell developing into you from the cell's perspective. Far too astronomical to get your head around, so we'll just look backwards and take it as a given so your head doesn't explode and make a mess of things. After all, we may still need some of you to successfully procreate.

Ok, math and statistics are fun, but they're not what this collection is about.

I never really knew my family… at least not beyond my immediate group of brothers and sisters, nieces and nephews. I knew my mom grew up in a lot of places, but considered herself from Salt Lake City where she was born. My dad came from a large family of farmers in Michigan. Sure, I had met a few cousins and aunts and uncles in my youth, but my grandparents all died long before I was born, and most of the rest of the family remained in Michigan whereas I was born and raised in California. When I was young, long-distance phone calls were expensive and I don't think either one of my parents liked to talk on the phone to begin with so it was extremely rare that I would ever hear my parents conversing with one of my mythical relatives back East, and my dad, not being an overly talkative person, rarely spoke of his family other than to tell a few tales of the kinds of trouble young farm boys would get into. So, other than a family reunion in Colorado when I was 10 or so, I never met most of them.

My parents were 40 when I was born and my Dad died at the age of 71. My Mom died last year at the age of 88. While she was alive, my Mom loved to tell my wife and I stories of her small circle of influential people: her mother, sister, step-fathers, boyfriends, and her Aunt Betty, but these were all strangers to me.

It was right about the same time that I became a middle-aged orphan that my wife and I started researching our genealogy. As reactivated members of the Church of Jesus Christ of Latter-day Saints, we received free access to Ancestry.com and FamilySearch.org and began to get interested in genealogy. "I'm not going to find much," I remember thinking. I'd be lucky if I could go back more than a couple of generations – after all, my kin were just poor Michigan farmers and my Mom's lineage was confusing and poorly documented at best.

Boy, was I wrong.

Within a few hours of playing with these web sites I found some amazing information, including:

I could trace the Sprague line back 600 years to the 1400's in Dorset, England. I always assumed we came from Germany. The Spragues lived for centuries in the village of Upwey. And some migrated to America in 1621, aboard the *Lyon's Whelp*, only a year or so after the original Mayflower settlers!

Our ancestral Spragues founded many settlements and towns, and two were governors of Rhode Island.

The comedienne Lucille Ball, my niece's idol, was proud of her Sprague heritage - being descended from the same English Spragues as we were. When I discovered this, I immediately called my niece to tell her the news.

My mom always talked about being Swiss-Irish, and I always thought Sprague was a German name. After I did the Ancestry.com DNA test, I was surprised to find we had almost zero Irish in us, but we did have quite a bit of Swiss, English, and French, and a little bit of Norwegian, German and Northern Italy. Truly a European cocktail... but almost no pure Irish.

Then, once I moved from Ancestry.com to FamilySearch.com, even more of my lineage opened up at an astounding pace. In one of my first sittings with FamilySearch.com I started exploring the interactive family tree... you click on one person and it opens up to show their parents. I wanted to see how far back I could go, so I began clicking in a "binary tree search" pattern (for you computer geeks) and things just kept going and going, until, about a 150 generations back I arrived at Adam! Yes, some of the early data is sketchy and there are seemingly incongruous gaps of times and some paths that start the same but lead to different destinations, but as the mysteries of thousands of years ago will never be solved, I just had to go with it. The other thing is that to get back this far, I navigated without any regard to whether I was following the maternal or paternal lines, I just wanted to follow whichever branch too me back the farthest. Depending on where other Sprague's intersect my line, this may or may not.

But here's the weird part... once I had done this, I wanted to write it down and it took me *hours*, and hundred and hundreds of clicks to again find the path that I had previously followed, almost without error or divergence. How in the world did I find that path so directly the first time? It almost seemed like an angel had guided my path. Like flipping a penny and calling the right heads or tails a hundred and fifty times in a row. However this came to be, I managed to find the path again and write it all down. The path took me through the US to England, to Duke William the First of Normandy, to France, to Emperor Charlemagne, and through Italian and Greek rulers, and down through the names familiar in the Bible; Abraham, Noah, Methuselah, Seth and Adam. What an amazing discovery that was. I suddenly felt like an integral part of the human story. It also amazed me to realize that there have only been something like 150 generations between us and Adam, a wee blip in the evolution of humankind. (You may be thinking, how can he use the term "evolution" and Adam in the same discussion. Here's what I believe: evolution is real and has been taking place for millions of years. Adam was not the first man-like creature on the Earth. Not by a long-shot. But he *may* have been the first homo-sapien to receive the divine spark of humanity, and from wence the rest of us descended. He's definitely the first in recorded history - whether you choose to believe that or not is up to you, but we have to start somewhere. Certainly attempting to trace your ancestry any farther back than Adam is pointless.) But this isn't a book of theology either…

Unfortunately, for the rest of you Spragues that are not part of my immediate family, I was only able to trace back to Adam through my mother's line. Doing the same binary tree search for the Sprague side resulted in wondrous results, but I never found the path "all the way" back. The best line I found for Sprague (again, following maternal as well as paternal lines), however, did take me back through King's of England, and back to Odin in 215AD.

Places

Sprague, Manitoba

Sprague is a community in the Canadian province of Manitoba minutes from Minnesota and Ontario. It is located in the Rural Municipality of Piney, about one hour southeast of Steinbach and 1.5 hours southeast of Winnipeg. It is a small town located at the junctions of Manitoba Highway 12 and Provincial Road 308. The nearest major centres include Warroad, Fort Frances, Steinbach, and Thief River Falls.

Sprague, Connecticut

Sprague is a town in New London County, Connecticut, United States. The town was named after William Sprague, who laid out the industrial section. The population was 2,984 at the 2010 census.

Location within New London County, Connecticut

Coordinates: 41°37′26″N 72°04′30″W

Country	United States
State	Connecticut
Incorporated	1861
Area	
• **Total**	13.8 sq mi (35.7 km^2)
• **Land**	13.2 sq mi (34.2 km^2)
• **Water**	0.6 sq mi (1.6 km^2)
Elevation	276 ft (84 m)
Population (2010)	
• **Total**	2,984
• **Density**	220/sq mi (84/km^2)
Website	www.ctsprague.org

Sprague is composed of three villages: Baltic, Hanover, and Versailles.

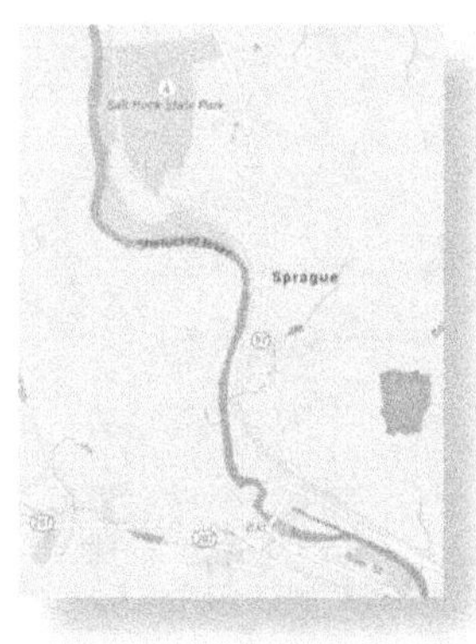
Sprague

ctsprague.org
Home
Town Hall
Boards & Commissions
Community
Events Calendar
Resources
About Sprague
Town of Sprague
Villages of Baltic, Hanover, Versailles
Town Hall Offices
1 Main Street
P.O. Box 677
Baltic, CT 06330
Phone: 860.822.3000
Fax: 860.822.3013
Hours
See Town Hall Offices
Welcome to Sprague
The perfect place to live and work in eastern Connecticut. Sprague is located right on the "border" between northeastern and southeastern Connecticut, within minutes of Rt. 395, and so is an easy (45 minutes) commute to the New London area, yet is also close (35 minutes) to both the University of Connecticut's Main Campus and Eastern Connecticut State University. Its three villages, Baltic, Hanover and Versailles, are rich in history, charm and architectural significance. The entire Baltic Village is listed on the National Register of Historic Places; Baltic was home to one of the largest textile mills in the country.

Sprague, Nebraska

Coordinates: 40°37′31″N 96°44′44″W	
Country	United States
State	Nebraska
County	Lancaster
Area	
• **Total**	0.10 sq mi (0.26 km²)
• **Land**	0.10 sq mi (0.26 km²)
• **Water**	0 sq mi (0 km²)
Elevation	1,280 ft (390 m)
Population (2010)	
• **Total**	142

Sprague is a village in Lancaster County, Nebraska, United States. It is part of the Lincoln, Nebraska Metropolitan Statistical Area. The population was 142 at the 2010 census. Sprague was established in 1888 when the Missouri Pacific Railroad was extended to that point.

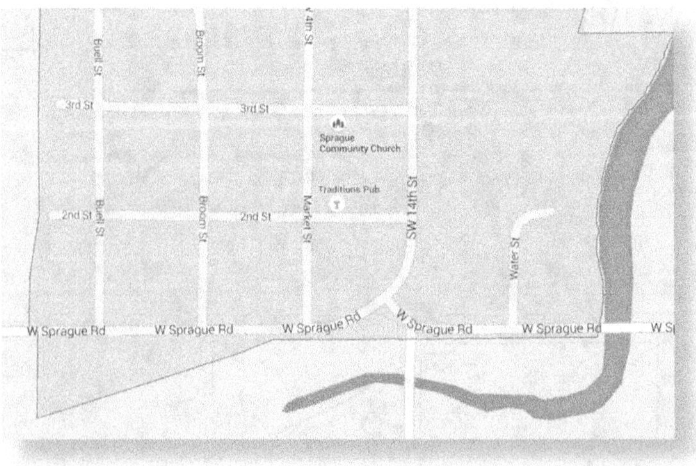

Sprague, Washington

Coordinates: 47°17′56″N 117°58′39″W	
Country	United States
State	Washington
County	Lincoln
Area	
• **Total**	0.63 sq mi (1.63 km²)
• **Land**	0.63 sq mi (1.63 km²)
• **Water**	0 sq mi (0 km²)
Elevation	1,903 ft (580 m)
Population (2010)	
• **Total**	446
• **Estimate** (2013)	429
• **Density**	707.9/sq mi (273.3/km²)

Sprague is a city in Lincoln County, Washington, United States. The population was 446 at the 2010 census. The town was plotted in 1880 and named for former American Civil War Union general John Wilson Sprague.

Eugene E. Lindsey, World War II naval hero, was born in Sprague.

History

Sprague was first settled by William Newman, who established an inn at the location.

Sprague was officially incorporated on November 28, 1883. Originally called Hoodooville after William Burrows, a local character called Hoodoo Billy, the name was changed to honor General John W. Sprague, a railroad executive.

Sprague was destroyed by fire on August 3, 1895.

Mary Queen of Heaven Catholic Church in Sprague, Washington was originally built in 1883. The current church was built in a Gothic Revival style and erected in 1902, just south of the site of the original church and blessed by the Bishop of Nesqually. It was placed on the National Register of Historic Places by the U.S. Department of Interior in 1990.

The town has a seasonal creek running through it named "Negro Creek." Much debate has occurred regarding the creek's name but the name remains.

The Sprague Catholic Cemetery

The Sprague Catholic Cemetery is associated with and maintained by the Mary Queen of Heaven Parish Church. Those buried in this historic cemetery include lifetime residents of Sprague as well as immigrants born as long ago as the 1850s. The first burial took place on December 25; Mr. and Mrs. Mike Ferrell buried their infant daughter Margaret Mabel Farrell. The Farrells later donated the plot of land their daughter was buried on to the Catholic Church. It was dedicated by Bishop Junger of Nesqually Diocese.

Sprague, Wisconsin

Coordinates:	44°08′52″N 90°07′53″W
Country	United States
State	Wisconsin
County	Juneau
Elevation	942 ft (287 m)

Sprague is an unincorporated community located in the town of Necedah, Juneau County, Wisconsin, United States. Sprague is located on Wisconsin Highway 80 and the Canadian National Railway 8.5 miles (13.7 km) north-northwest of the village of Necedah.

Sprague River, Oregon

Coordinates:	42°27′20″N 121°30′11″W
Country	United States
State	Oregon
County	Klamath
Elevation	4,354 ft (1,327 m)

Sprague River is an unincorporated community in Klamath County, Oregon, United States. It is located about 45 miles (72 km) northeast of Klamath Falls near the Sprague River, northwest of Oregon Route 140.

History

The Sprague River was named for Captain Franklin B. Sprague, who participated in the Snake and Paiute Indian wars, and was in command of Fort Klamath in 1866. His name was applied to the river by 1864, and perhaps earlier. The Klamath name for the stream was *Plai* or *Plaikni Koke*. *Koke* was the generic word for "river" and *plai* meant the river came from upper or higher country.

Sprague River post office, named after the stream, was established September 14, 1923, with Benjamin E. Wolford as the first postmaster. There was an earlier post office named Sprague River much farther east and upstream of the current community. The Oregon, California and Eastern Railway had a station nearby. The former rail line is now the OC&E Woods Line State Trail.

At one time there was a sawmill and a box factory in the community.

Sprague Field

Sprague Field is a multi-purpose stadium in Montclair, New Jersey on the campus of Montclair State University. It holds 5,700 people. Major League Lacrosse's New Jersey Pride hosted their home games at this stadium from 2004 to 2005.

Sprague River (Oregon)

Name origin: Capt. F.B. Sprague, commander of Fort Klamath in 1866	
Country	United States
State	Oregon
County	Klamath
Source	Confluence of the Sprague River's north and south forks
- location	near Bly, Klamath County, Oregon
- elevation	4,325 ft (1,318 m)
- coordinates	42°26′16″N 121°06′34″W
Mouth	Williamson River
- location	Chiloquin, Klamath County, Oregon
- elevation	4,163 ft (1,269 m)
Basin	1,565 sq mi (4,053 km^2)
Discharge	for 1 mile (1.6 km) northeast of Chiloquin, 5.4 miles (8.7 km) from mouth
- average	580 cu ft/s (16 m^3/s)
- max	14,900 cu ft/s (422 m^3/s)
- min	50 cu ft/s (1 m^3/s)

The **Sprague River** is a tributary of the Williamson River, approximately 75 miles (121 km) long, in southwestern Oregon in the United States. It drains an arid volcanic plateau region east of the Cascade Range in the watershed of the Klamath River.

It is formed by the confluence of its north and south forks in eastern Klamath County, approximately 35 miles (56 km) east-northeast of Klamath Falls at 42.437650°N 121.109435°W. The **North Fork Sprague River**, 30 miles (48 km), rises in southwestern Lake County in the Fremont National Forest near Gearhart Mountain at 42.5287618°N 120.8183115°W and flows southwest. The **South Fork Sprague River**, 30 miles (48 km), rises northeast of Quartz Mountain Pass at 42.4815400°N 120.7869201°W and flows west-northwest. The combined stream flows west through the broad Sprague Valley, past the small communities of Bly, Beatty, and Sprague River. It joins the Williamson from the east at Chiloquin, about

10 miles (16 km) north of the mouth of the Williamson on Upper Klamath Lake at 42.5712475°N 121.8744593°W.
It receives the Sycan River from the north at Beatty. Superb trout fishing exists in the Sprague and its tributaries.

Sprague River (Maine)

The **Sprague River** is a 2.5-mile-long (4.0 km) river in the town of Phippsburg, Maine. It flows primarily through tidal marsh and empties into the Atlantic Ocean, 1.5 miles (2.4 km) west of the mouth of the Morse River and 3.5 miles (5.6 km) west of the mouth of the Kennebec River.

Sprague Road, Groveland, CA

Sprague Road crosses Highway 120 four times east of Groveland, California, on the way to Yosemite National Park.

Random Point of Interest

People

Surname

- Achsa W. Sprague (1827–1862), American spiritualist
- Bud Sprague (1904–1973), American footballer
- Carl T. Sprague (1895-1979), American country musician
- Charles Sprague (1791 - 1875)
- Clifton Sprague, American admiral during World War II
- David Sprague (1910–1968), Canadian footballer
- E. Carleton Sprague (1822–1895), New York lawyer and politician
- Ed Sprague, Sr., former Major League Baseball pitcher
- Ed Sprague, Jr., former Major League Baseball third baseman, and son of the pitcher
- Edward Spragge (AKA Spragg or Sprague, c.1620–73), Irish admiral of the Royal Navy
- Elmer Sprague, American philosopher
- Erik Sprague (born 1972), the self-styled Lizardman, a freak show and sideshow performer
- Ernest Sprague (1865–1938), American footballer, public official, and engineer
- Frank J. Sprague (1857–1934), American naval officer and inventor, notable for development

of electric machinery

- Frank Lee Sprague, American guitarist and composer
- George Sprague (1871-1963), American businessman and mayor of Dallas
- Franklin B. Sprague (1825–1895), American military officer, businessman, and judge
- Isaac Sprague, botanical illustrator
- Isaac W. Sprague (1841-1887), the *Original Thin Man*, an American "human skeleton"
- J. Russell Sprague (1886–1969), American politician
- Jack Sprague, the only 3-time NASCAR Craftsman Truck Series Champion
- Jake Sprague (born 1984), American rugby union player
- Jo Ann Sprague (born 1931), former Massachusetts State Representative and State Senator
- John Allison Sprague (born 1844), Ontario farmer and politician
- John W. Sprague (1817–1894), American soldier and railroad executive
- Ken Sprague, political cartoonist
- Lucian Sprague, American railroad executive
- Martyn Sprague (born 1949), Welsh former professional footballer
- Peleg Sprague (Maine politician), politician from the state of Maine
- Peleg Sprague (New Hampshire), politician from the state of New Hampshire

- Peter Sprague (born 1955), American jazz musician
- Richard Sprague (1921–1996), American computer technician, researcher and author
- Robert C. Sprague (1900–1991), American Air Force Undersecretary, inventor and founder of Sprague Electric
- Roderick Sprague (born 1933), American anthropologist, ethnohistorian and historical archaeologist
- R. B. Sprague (1937–2010), American Contemporary Realist artist
- Royal Sprague, 11th Chief Justice of the Supreme Court of California
- Thomas Bond Sprague (1830–1920), British actuary
- Thomas L. Sprague, American vice admiral in WWII
- William Sprague

First name

- Sprague Cleghorn, former NHL hockey player
- Sprague Grayden, American actress (born 1980)

Middle name

- L. Sprague de Camp, author

Achsa W. Sprague

Achsa W. Sprague (November 17, 1827 - July 6, 1862) was one of the best-known Spiritualists during the 1850s in the United States. Primarily a medium and trance lecturer, she also wrote articles and poetry for Spiritualist publications such as the *Banner of Light*, the *Green Mountain Sibyl*, and the *People's World*.

Sprague was born at Plymouth Notch, Vermont. An able student, she began teaching other children at age 12. In 1847, at the age of 20, she became ill with rheumatic fever and credited her eventual recovery in 1854 to intercession by spirits. Between 1854 and her death in 1861 she traveled about the United States and Canada, entering into trances before audiences and speaking with the voices of alleged spirits. Like most Spiritualists of the time, she was an abolitionist and an advocate of women's rights. Sprague's papers are archived in the library of the Vermont Historical Society.

Bud Sprague

Date of birth:	September 8, 1904
Place of birth:	Dallas, Texas
Date of death:	April 25, 1973 (aged 68)
Place of death:	New York, New York

Mortimer 'Bud' Sprague (September 8, 1904 - April 25, 1973) was an American football player. He was elected to the College Football Hall of Fame in 1970.

He was one of the eight children born to Minna and George Sprague, of the Oak Cliff neighborhood in Dallas, Texas. Bud's father George served on the Dallas City Council and as the Mayor of Dallas from 1937 to 1939. Bud originally played on University of Texas' varsity football team, and later transferred to the United States Military Academy to play out his eligibility for the Army Black Knights. Eventually Bud settled in the Greenwich Village neighborhood of Manhattan and made his fortune in maritime insurance. He named his son, Kurth Sprague, after his mentor[.

Carl T. Sprague

Carl T. "Doc" Sprague (May 10, 1895 - February 21, 1979) was an American country musician. He was often dubbed "The Original Singing Cowboy". Sprague was one of the first country musicians on record, recording in the early 1920s.

Sprague grew up on a farm near Houston, Texas and learned traditional cowboy songs as a child. During his college years at Texas A&M, he played in a band and, later on, worked as an athletic trainer. He also found time to conduct a weekly radio program on campus. Sprague served in World War I. He graduated from college in 1922 and was offered occasional work performing on radio. He received a recording contract by Victor in 1925. In August, the same year, he went to Camden, New Jersey to record his first ten songs. His debut sides were "When the Work's All Done This Fall" and "Bad Companions"; the former would go on to sell over 900,000 copies. His recording of "The Dying Cowboy" became a hit in 1926. Other successful recordings were "The Boston Burglar" and "The Two Soldiers." He recorded with Victor until 1929, releasing 33 songs. In the 1930s he moved to Bryan, Texas and ceased recording, though he would return to play folk festivals during the genre's resurgence in the 1950s and 1960s. He died in 1979 in Bryan, Texas.

Charles Sprague (poet)

Charles Sprague (October 26, 1791 - January 22, 1875) was an early American poet. He worked for 45 years for the State and Globe Banks and was often referred to as the "Banker Poet of Boston". His odes and prologues won several competitive prizes and were collected and published in 1841 as *The Writings of Charles Sprague*.

He was born in Boston on October 26, 1791. He was a descendant of some of America's founding fathers, including his father, Samuel Sprague (participant in the Boston Tea Party and Revolutionary War), Richard Warren (Mayflower passenger) and the Reverend Peter Hobart and William Sprague of Hingham. He received a common-school education, beginning at age 10 at the Franklin School[*disambiguation needed* in Boston. He was taught by Dr. Asa Bullard and Mr. Lemuel Shaw who later became Chief Justice of the Massachusetts Supreme Judicial Court. He lost the use of his left eye by an accident at age 10.

His formal education ended at thirteen when he was apprenticed to a dry goods merchant, Messrs Thayer and Hunt. Here he gained his first practical knowledge of business. Later he formed a co-partnership with William B. Collander in the grocery business. He married Elizabeth Rand in 1814 and had four children, two dying in childhood. In 1819 be began working for the State Bank as a teller and when the Globe Bank was established in 1824 was employed there as a cashier. He remained there, becoming an officer in the institution, until 1865 and was often referred to as the "Banker Poet" of Boston. He resigned his bank position, when at 73 years and growing infirm with age, he didn't want to undertake the labors of a new regime of banking under national laws. He enjoyed the comforts of home life, surrounded by his books, until January 22, 1875, when after a short illness he died at 84.

His first recognition for poetry came when he won a prize for the best prologue at the opening of the Park Theater in New York. His first printed efforts were published in the *Centennial, Boston Gazette,* and *The Evening Gazette* as early as 1811. Upon the occasion of the triumphal entry of Lafayette into Boston, in 1824, he wrote the inscription for an arch that hung over the streets of Boston.

Many of Charles Sprague's poems were delivered at public festivities – major, historical Boston events – including *Curiosity*, delivered at the Phi Beta Kappa Society of Harvard University in 1829. This is his longest and most elaborate work. In the *Salem Observer*, August 29, 1829, it is noted that at the commencement at Harvard an honorary degree of Master of Arts was given to Mr. Charles Sprague, the poet. It goes on to state, "We are glad that the distributors of the literary honors of old Harvard are so discriminating in the selection of the candidates for their favors". This was quite an accomplishment as his formal education ended at thirteen and he was the epitome of a 'self-made' man. "Shakespeare Ode" was delivered at a Boston theatre in a pageant in honor of Shakespeare, in 1823; "Ode" was pronounced at the Centennial Celebration of the Settlement of Boston of 1830; "Triennial Ode" at the Massachusetts Charitable Assoc. 1818; "Fifty Years Ago" at the Fourth of July Celebration, and "Song" at a festival in Faneuil Hall.

Charles A. Sprague

Charles A. Sprague

22nd Governor of Oregon	
In office	
January 12, 1939 – January 9, 1943	
Preceded by	Charles H. Martin
Personal details	
Born	November 12, 1887 Lawrence, Kansas
Died	March 13, 1969 (aged 81) Salem, Oregon
Political party	Republican
Spouse(s)	Blanche Chamberlain
Profession	Politician

Charles Arthur Sprague, (November 12, 1887 - March 13, 1969) was the 22nd Governor of the US state of Oregon from 1939 to 1943. He was also the editor and publisher of the Oregon Statesman from 1929 to 1969. Sprague High School in Salem, Oregon is named after him.

He was also distantly related to two Rhode Island Governors, William Sprague III and William Sprague IV.

Early years

Charles Sprague was born in Lawrence, Kansas, as the son of Charles Allen Sprague, a grain-elevator operator, and Caroline Glasgow. He grew up with his brother, Robert Wyatt, in Columbus Junction, Iowa, where he attended public schools and worked for his father. He enrolled at Monmouth College in Illinois and paid his expenses by reporting part-time for regional newspapers. When his income proved inadequate, Sprague took a leave at the end of his sophomore year and spent two years as a high school principal and teacher in Ainsworth, Iowa. On his return to Monmouth, Sprague served as editor of the student newspaper. From then on, he had aspirations to go into journalism. Following his graduation with honors in 1910, Sprague became superintendent of schools in Waitsburg, Washington. Two years later, he married Blanche Chamberlain, the principal of a local grade school; they had two children. Sprague was soon named assistant superintendent of public instruction for the state of Washington.

Becomes a public figure

In 1925 he acquired a one-third interest in the became the business manager of the Corvallis Gazette Times, and four years later, purchased a two-thirds interest in the Oregon Statesman, long the most influential newspaper in the capital city of Salem. For the next forty years, he was its editor and publisher. In 1955 Sprague received the Elijah Parish Lovejoy Award as well as an honorary Doctor of Laws degree from Colby College. Sprague established himself as one of the leading editorialists and public commentators of the Pacific Northwest, and his editorials were often reprinted in some of America's largest newspapers. Sprague gained a national reputation as an articulate spokesman for small-town values, fiscal conservatism, and internationalism. He held control of the paper until his death. A declared Republican, he nonetheless took an independent position on the issues of the time, reflecting a progressive view which was often at odds with leaders of his party.

In 1938 Republicans were hesitant to challenge the Democratic incumbent governor Charles H. Martin, who had strong Republican business support. As a result Sprague easily won the Republican nomination for governor in a field of eight candidates. In the meantime, however, Martin was a New Deal critic and was opposed in his own primary by the Roosevelt administration's choice, State Senator Henry Hess. Taking advantage of the split among the Democrats, Sprague made the administrations' intervention a major campaign theme, urging voters to "repudiate outside interference in local affairs." Martin and his allies campaigned for Sprague. Sprague won decisively, carrying 32 of the 36 counties in the general election, winning 214,062 votes to Hess' 158,744. Republicans also won control of the Oregon State Senate, 21 to 9, and the House, 50 to 10.

Term as governor

As governor, Sprague invoked the populist legacy of George W. Joseph and Julius Meier. With backing from both labor and industry, he moved quickly to improve the state's employment services and launched vocational-training programs to aid the jobless in efforts to lift Oregon out of the Great Depression. He modernized the state school system by pushing through legislation that provided for the consolidation of rural school districts. He reduced the state debt by $12 million and balanced the budget while increasing social welfare services. Sprague helped maintain peace in labor disputes by his forthright opposition to an antipicketing law that was later held to be unconstitutional by the Oregon Supreme Court. He lost the political backing of organized labor, though, as a result of his policy of awarding state contracts to the lowest bidder, whether or not they were union firms.

Republicans expected smooth sailing legislatively and politically. Nevertheless, he vetoed so many special interest bills passed by his fellow Republicans that opponents initiated a recall move. It failed, but Sprague's effectiveness had been reduced.

During Sprague's administration, Oregon became the first state to initiate control over logging operations to insure enforcement of progressive forest practices. These practices included reasonable protection of trees from slash burns, not harvesting immature trees during cutting operations, and retaining some mature trees for seeding purposes. In addition, a state forestry research program was adopted. He also established a forestry research program and obtained authority for the state to acquire abandoned cut over land for replanting. "Wise handling of natural forest lands," he declared, "calls for their consolidation under public ownership except for those lands in the hands of strong private interests capable of carrying them through long growing periods."

After one term, Sprague was defeated for the 1942 Oregon Republican gubernatorial nomination by the Secretary of State, Earl Snell, who went on to be elected Governor.

Death & Remembrance

Sprague died on March 13, 1969. Sprague and his wife are interred in Mount Crest Abbey Mausoleum, in Salem, Oregon.

The Salem-Keizer School District named Charles A. Sprague High School, known as Sprague High School, in his honor in 1972.

Charles Ezra Sprague

Charles Ezra Sprague (October 9, 1842 - March 21, 1912) was an American accountant, born in Nassau, Rensselaer County, New York. He was known as a Civil War hero, and as a proponent of the constructed language Volapük, for which he authored the first major textbook in English, *Handbook of Volapük* (1888), as well as an early organizer of the accounting profession.

During the Civil War, Sprague served in the 44th New York Infantry, seeing action at the Battle of Gettysburg, where his unit was instrumental in helping repulse attacks on Little Round Top.

He was president of both the New York Institute of Accounts and the Union Dime Savings Bank (which later became the Dime Savings Bank). Later in life, he was involved in the movement for reform of English spelling as part of the Simplified Spelling Board, of which he was the first treasurer.

He was heavily involved in the development of the first state certification of accountants in the United States. In 1953 he was inducted into Ohio State University's Accounting Hall of Fame.
Sprague was the maternal grandfather of science fiction author L. Sprague de Camp.

Charles F. Sprague

Member of the U.S. House of Representatives from Massachusetts's 11th district	
In office	
March 4, 1897 – March 3, 1901	
Member of the Massachusetts State Senate	
Ninth Suffolk District	
In office	
January, 1895 - January, 1897	
Personal details	
Born	June 10, 1857 Boston, Massachusetts
Died	January 30, 1902 (aged 44) Providence, Rhode Island
Resting place	Mount Auburn Cemetery
Political party	Republican
Spouse(s)	Mary Bryant Pratt
Alma mater	Harvard, Harvard Law School
Profession	Attorney

Charles Franklin Sprague (June 10, 1857 – January 30, 1902) was a U.S. Representative from Massachusetts, grandson of Peleg Sprague (1793–1880).

Born in Boston, Massachusetts, Sprague attended the public schools and was graduated from Harvard University in 1879. He studied law at the Harvard Law School and the Boston University and was admitted to the bar in Boston. He served as member of the Boston Common Council in 1889 and 1890. He served as member of the Massachusetts House of

Representatives in 1891 and 1892. He served as chairman of the board of park commissioners of the city of Boston in 1893 and 1894. Sprague served in the State senate in 1895 and 1896.

Sprague was elected as a Republican to the Fifty-fifth and Fifty-sixth Congresses (March 4, 1897-March 3, 1901). He declined to be a candidate for renomination in 1900 to the Fifty-seventh Congress. He died in the Butler Sanitarium in Providence, Rhode Island, on January 30, 1902. He was interred in Mount Auburn Cemetery, Watertown, Massachusetts.

Charlie Sprague

Charlie Sprague, Chicago White Stockings, Pitcher, Old Judge Cigarettes	
Pitcher	
Born: October 10, 1864 Cleveland, Ohio	
Died: December 31, 1912 (aged 48) Des Moines, Iowa	
Batted: Left	**Threw:** Left
MLB debut	
September 17, 1887 for the Chicago White Stockings	
Last MLB appearance	
October 10, 1890 for the Toledo Maumees	
Career statistics	
Win-Loss Record	10-7
E.R.A.	4.51
Strikeouts	76
Teams	
Chicago White Stockings (1887) Cleveland Spiders (1889) Toledo Maumees (1890)	

Charlie Sprague (October 10, 1864 in Cleveland, Ohio – December 31, 1912 in Des Moines, Iowa) was an outfielder and pitcher for Major League Baseball in the 19th century.

Clifton Sprague

Nickname(s)	"*Ziggy*"
Born	January 8, 1896 Dorchester, Boston, Massachusetts
Died	April 11, 1955 (aged 59) San Diego, California
Place of burial	Fort Rosecrans National Cemetery
Allegiance	United States of America
Service/branch	United States Navy
Years of service	1914–1951
Rank	Vice Admiral
Commands	Aircraft Squadron 3

held	USS *Patoka* (AO-9) USS *Tangier* (AV-8) USS *Wasp* (CV-18) Carrier Division 25 Carrier Division 26 Carrier Division 2 Navy Air Group 1.6 Carrier Division 6
Battles/wars	World War I World War II
Awards	Navy Cross Legion of Merit (4)

Vice Admiral **Clifton Albert Frederick ("Ziggy") Sprague** (January 8, 1896 – April 11, 1955) was a World War II-era officer in the United States Navy.

Biography

Sprague was born in Dorchester, Massachusetts, and attended the Roxbury Latin School, and the United States Naval Academy in June 1914. There he was given the nickname "Ziggy" (although no relation to Admiral Thomas L. Sprague, the two both attended the Naval Academy, later graduating from the same class). Due to the American involvement in World War I he received his commission as an ensign one year early on June 28, 1917, finishing forty-third out of 199. His wife was the sister of *The Great Gatsby* author F. Scott Fitzgerald.

World War I

His first assignment was on the gunboat *Wheeling* (PG-14) where he served as Gunnery Officer, Communications Officer,

Navigator, and Executive Officer. *Wheeling* served as a convoy escort in the Atlantic and Mediterranean during the war. While assigned to *Wheeling* he was promoted to lieutenant (junior grade) and lieutenant. After the war in October 1919, Sprague was assigned as the reserve Commanding Officer of the destroyer *Manley* (DD-74) for two months. Thereafter he was assigned to the new battleship *Tennessee* (BB-43) and served as 6th Broadside Battery Officer for one year.

1920 to 1940 - Naval Aviator

On December 3, 1920, Sprague joined 33 other classmates at Naval Air Station Pensacola, Florida as a student pilot. His first flight was on January 11, 1921, when he piloted a Curtiss N-9 aircraft for twenty minutes. Sprague earned the designation Naval Aviator No. 2934 on August 11, 1921. Due to his great proficiency within two months he was designated as Commanding Officer of Aircraft Squadron 3 at Pensacola.

From March 1922 to November 1923, Sprague was assigned to Aircraft Squadron VS-1 with the Atlantic Fleet based on the seaplane tender *Wright*. He reported to his next duty station Naval Air Station Anacostia, near Washington, D.C., in November 1923 where he served as a Test Pilot, Operations Officer, and Executive Officer. As a Test Pilot he conducted experimental and research work at the Naval Aircraft Factory in Philadelphia, Pennsylvania, in 1923, where he contributed to the development of aircraft carrier catapult systems. From March 1926 to February 1928 he assisted inventor Carl Norden in the laboratory and as a Test Pilot at Naval Air Station Hampton Roads, Virginia, with improvements to the Mark-1 aircraft carrier arresting gear system for *Lexington* (CV-2) and *Saratoga* (CV-3).
Sprague reported to *Lexington* in March 1928 where he assumed the duties of Flight Deck Officer and Assistant Air

Officer. In January 1929 *Lexington* along with *Langley* and *Saratoga* participated in Fleet Problem IX, a simulated aerial attack on the Panama Canal. Sprague's tour on *Lexington* ended in April 1929. Returning to the U.S. Naval Academy in May 1929 Sprague served as Executive Officer of VN-8-D5. On June 10, 1930 he was promoted to lieutenant commander. His tour at the Naval Academy ended in November 1931.

Sprague served as Squadron Commander of VP-8 in Panama in December 1931 to April 1934. The squadron was based on the seaplane tender *Wright* (AV-1) homeported at the Norfolk Navy Yard. In 1933 the squadron was moved to Hawaii where Sprague became the first Navy Pilot to fly a thirteen-hour round-trip from Hawaii to Midway Island in February 1934. From May 1934 to July 1936, Sprague served as Air Operations Officer at Naval Air Station Norfolk, Virginia, where his department serviced several aircraft carrier squadrons.

In July 1936, Sprague was assigned to the newly constructed aircraft carrier *Yorktown* (CV-5) as Air Officer. After her commissioning, he piloted the first two landings ever made on *Yorktown*. In addition, he was the first pilot to test the catapult system on *Yorktown*. Sprague was promoted to commander in December 1937. He spent all of 1938 managing the Air Department and aircraft squadrons on *Yorktown*. In February 1939 *Yorktown* participated in Fleet Problem XX in the Caribbean. Shortly thereafter Sprague left the carrier in June 1939. Sprague was ordered to the Naval War College in Newport, Rhode Island, in June 1939 where he spent three months in study before reporting to his first sea command, the 21-year old oil tanker *Patoka* (AO-9) at Puget Sound Naval Shipyard, Bremerton, Washington. Sprague commanded *Patoka* until June 1940 when he was sent back to the Naval War College for two more months of study.

World War II

At Oakland, California, Sprague took command of the cargo ship *Tangier* (AV-8) which was being converted into a seaplane tender in July 1940. *Tangier* was commissioned on August 25, 1941 and shortly thereafter transited to Bremerton, Washington to load torpedoes. At her homeport in Pearl Harbor, Hawaii, *Tangier* was mated with Fleet Patrol Wing Two. *Tangier* was berthed at F-10 on the Northwest side of Ford Island on the morning of December 7, 1941. She was one of the first ships in the harbor to open fire and engaged several Japanese aircraft throughout the morning. *Tangier* was credited with downing three aircraft. As a result of his leadership at Pearl Harbor, Sprague was promoted to captain on January 3, 1942. In early 1942 *Tangier* saw service at New Caledonia.
Sprague was assigned as Air Officer of Gulf Sea Frontier, Miami, Florida in June 1942. His duties involved improving defenses, keeping the sea lanes open, and countering the German U-boats on the Southeast coast of the United States. Upon achieving his goals he was transferred in March 1943. In April 1943, Sprague was transferred to Naval Air Center, Seattle, Washington, where he served as Commander of the base and nearby Naval Air Station Sand Point. This duty ended abruptly when he was assigned as the Commanding Officer of the newly constructed fast fleet carrier *Wasp* (CV-18) in October 1943.

Arriving at Bethlehem Steel Company Fore River Yard near Boston, Massachusetts, Sprague took command of *Wasp* where she was commissioned on November 24, 1943. The carrier was quickly sent to the Pacific where she joined the war against the Japanese. Her first combat missions were to destroy enemy aircraft, installations, and surface craft on Marcus and Wake Islands in May 1944. In June 1944 *Wasp* participated in the invasion of Saipan and the Battle of the Philippine Sea. On

July 9, 1944, shortly before leaving *Wasp*, Sprague was promoted to rear admiral at age 48.

Sprague was designated as Commander Carrier Division 25 on July 23, 1944 with his flag in *Fanshaw Bay* (CVE-70), replacing Rear Admiral Gerald F. Bogan. In September 1944 his Task Unit supported the Morotai landing.

Sprague's greatest achievement came on October 25, 1944 when his Task Unit 77.4.3 (Taffy III) consisting of 6 escort carriers, 3 destroyers, and 4 destroyer escorts fought off the vastly superior Japanese Center Force at the Battle off Samar. The Japanese force consisted of 4 battleships, 6 heavy cruisers, 2 light cruisers, and 11 destroyers off the Samar Island in the Philippines. The Taffy CVE pilots bombed, strafed, and made dry runs while the Destroyers first laid smoke to cover the carriers, then made torpedo runs on the battleships and cruisers of Center Force then fought toe-to-toe gun duels with them. For the leadership he displayed in this incident, he received the Navy Cross.

On February 19, 1945, Sprague assumed command of Carrier Division 26 embarked on *Natoma Bay* (CVE-62) for the invasion of Iwo Jima where his unit provided close air support for the Marines ashore. The next month he moved his flag back to *Fanshaw Bay* for the invasion of Okinawa. In April 1945, Sprague was given command of Carrier Division 2, a fast carrier Task Group and moved his flag to *Ticonderoga* (CV-14) on June 1, 1945. His Task Group operated against the Japanese home islands of Kyūshū, Honshū, and Hokkaidō. Sprague received the notification of the end of hostilities while steaming 151 miles off the eastern coast of Honsh□ on August 15, 1945. Four days after the Japanese surrender, Sprague and *Ticonderoga* entered Tokyo Bay.

Post War - Operation Crossroads

Memorial to Sprague next to the USS *Midway* in San Diego.

Sprague returned to the West Coast onboard *Bennington* (CV-20) in November 1945. He spent the next month in Washington, D.C. briefing Naval leaders at the White House. In February 1946, Sprague was given command of Navy Air Group 1.6 of Joint Task Force 1 with his flag in *Shangri-La* (CV-38) at San Diego, California. During the next six months he supported the naval aviation forces in Operation Crossroads nuclear tests on Bikini Atoll in the Marshall Islands.
At Corpus Christi, Texas, Sprague was assigned as Chief of Naval Air Basic Training in August 1946. In January 1948 he was redesignated as Commander, Naval Air Advanced Training. His tour ended in April 1948. Sprague's last seagoing command was as Commander, Carrier Division 6 with his flag in *Kearsarge* (CV-33) from May to October 1948.

During this tour *Kearsarge* operated in the Mediterranean. On January 1, 1949 to February 1950, Sprague was Commander of Naval Air Bases, Eleventh and Twelfth Naval District at Naval Air Station Coronado in San Diego, California. Reassigned in March 1950, Sprague was moved to Alaska where he served as Commandant, Seventeenth Naval District and Commander, Alaskan Sea Frontier on Kodiak Island. It was from here that he embarked on a B-29 and became the first U.S. Navy admiral to fly over the North Pole on November 12, 1950.

Retirement and death

On August 9, 1951, Sprague requested voluntary retirement from the Navy and was officially retired on November 1, 1951. As was custom at the time, he was advanced to vice admiral at retirement in recognition of his Navy Cross. He had spent 34 years, 4 months, and 4 days on active duty. In March 1955, Sprague fell ill of a weak heart and was moved to the Naval Hospital, San Diego, California. On April 11, 1955, 59-year-old Sprague died from a massive heart attack. Two days later he was buried at Fort Rosecrans National Cemetery at Point Loma, San Diego, California.

Decorations

The ribbon bar of Vice Admiral Clifton Sprague:

Namesake

The *Oliver Hazard Perry*-class guided-missile frigate USS *Clifton Sprague* (FFG-16) was named after Vice Admiral Sprague. The unclassified citation for the Navy Cross was in the wardroom until shortly before decommissioning.

E. Carleton Sprague

Eben Carleton Sprague (November 28, 1822 - February 14, 1895) was an American lawyer and politician from New York.

He born on November 28, 1822, in Bath, Grafton County, New Hampshire, the son of Noah Paul Sprague (1798–1879) and Abiah (Carlton) Sprague. He attended Phillips Exeter Academy, and graduated from Harvard College in 1843. Then he studied law with Millard Fillmore and Solomon G. Haven, was admitted to the bar in 1846, and practiced in Buffalo. On June 25, 1849, he married Elizabeth Hubbard Williams (1831–1908), and they had eight children.

He was a member of the New York State Senate (31st D.) in 1877.
He was Chancellor of the University of Buffalo from 1885 until his death in 1895.

He died on February 14, 1895, in Buffalo, New York.

Ed Sprague, Sr.

Pitcher	
Born: September 16, 1945 (age 69) Boston, Massachusetts	
Batted: Right	**Threw:** Right
MLB debut	
April 10, 1968 for the Oakland Athletics	
Last MLB appearance	

June 5, 1976 for the Milwaukee Brewers	
Career statistics	
Win–loss record	17–23
Earned run average	3.84
Strikeouts	188
Teams	
Oakland Athletics (1968–1969) Cincinnati Reds (1971–1973) St. Louis Cardinals (1973) Milwaukee Brewers (1973–1976)	

Edward Nelson Sprague, Sr. (born September 16, 1945) is a former professional baseball pitcher. He played all or part of eight seasons in Major League Baseball for four different teams between 1968 and 1976. Listed at 6 ft 4 in (1.93 m), 195 lb., he batted and threw right-handed.

Sprague is a 1963 graduate of Sunset High School (Hayward, California).

A hard-thrower, Sprague was scouted while pitching in the U.S. Army in Germany and was signed by the St. Louis Cardinals in 1966. A year later he was sold to the Oakland Athletics. He entered the majors in 1968 with the Athletics, playing for them until 1969 before joining the Cincinnati Reds (1971–73), St. Louis Cardinals (1973) and Milwaukee Brewers (1973–76). He filled various pitching roles as a closer and a middle reliever and as an occasional starter. His most productive season came in 1974 with Milwaukee, when he set career-highs in wins (7), strikeouts (57) and earned run average (2.39) in 20 games, including 10 as a starter, before damaging knee ligaments which ended his season.

In an eight-season career, Sprague posted a 17–23 record with

188 strikeouts and a 3.84 ERA in 198 games, including 23 starts, three complete games, nine saves and 408.0 innings pitched.

Following his playing career, Sprague became the owner of the Stockton Ports and his wife the owner of the Lodi Crushers. His son, Ed Jr., was the Toronto Blue Jays' first pick in the 1988 draft and played in the majors from 1991 to 2001.

Ed Sprague, Jr.

Third baseman	
Born: July 25, 1967 (age 47) Castro Valley, California	
Batted: Right	**Threw:** Right
MLB debut	
May 8, 1991 for the Toronto Blue Jays	
Last MLB appearance	
October 7, 2001 for the Seattle Mariners	
Career statistics	
Batting average	.247
Home runs	152
Runs batted in	558
Teams	
Toronto Blue Jays (1991–1998) Oakland Athletics (1998) Pittsburgh Pirates (1999) San Diego Padres (2000) Boston Red Sox (2000) Seattle Mariners (2001)	

Career highlights and awards
• All-Star (1999) • 2× World Series champion (1992, 1993)

Medal record	
Baseball	
Competitor for the United States	
Olympic Games	
1988 Seoul	Team
Baseball World Cup	
1988 Rome	Team

Edward Nelson Sprague, Jr. (born July 25, 1967) is a former Major League Baseball third baseman. He played 11 seasons in the major leagues from 1991 to 2001, with six different teams. He is currently the head baseball coach of the NCAA's Pacific Tigers.

College career and Olympics

Sprague was an NCAA standout where he played third base helping Stanford win College World Series championships in 1987 and 1988. He then collected an Olympic Gold Medal in the 1988 Olympics on the men's baseball team. (However, because baseball was a demonstration sport that year, the medals were unofficial and did not count towards respective countries' medal counts.) He is a member of Delta Tau Delta International Fraternity.

Sprague was drafted in the first round of the 1988 Major League Baseball Draft by the Toronto Blue Jays.

Major league career

Sprague made his debut in 1991 for the Toronto Blue Jays and was a part of the 1992 and 1993 World Series championships. He is particularly remembered for hitting the game-winning home run in the ninth inning of Game 2 of the 1992 Series against the Atlanta Braves. His best individual year came in 1996 when he hit .247 with 36 home runs and 101 runs batted in.

Sprague was a regular with Toronto until 1998, when he was traded to the Oakland Athletics. He was granted free agency at the end of 1998, and then played for the Pittsburgh Pirates in 1999, for which he made his only All-Star game appearance. That year, he hit .267 with 22 homers, 81 RBI and a .352 on-base percentage, the best of his career as a regular player.

In 2000, Sprague played for the San Diego Padres and Boston Red Sox. After becoming a free agent at the end of the year, he signed with the Seattle Mariners for the 2001 season, playing in 45 regular season games. He signed a minor league contract with the Texas Rangers in early 2002, but did not return to the major leagues.

Sprague twice led the league in getting hit by pitches and finished with a career total of 91. Sprague is the only baseball player ever to win championships in the College World Series, the Olympics, and the World Series.

Sprague's final career totals include 1203 games played, 506 runs, 1010 hits, 225 doubles, 12 triples, 152 home runs, 558 runs batted in, a .247 batting average, a .318 on-base average, and a .419 slugging average.

According to a report in the Stockton Record, Sprague said he used performance-enhancing substances later banned by

Major League Baseball and admitted hitting a home run with a corked bat.

Coaching career

Sprague has been the head coach of the Pacific Tigers college baseball team since the start of the 2004 season.

Personal life

Sprague and his wife Kristen Babb-Sprague, who is an Olympic Gold Medalist in synchronized swimming, have four children. Their daughter Payton attends the University of Wisconsin-Madison School of Business and their son Jed plays baseball at University of the Pacific. Jed was selected by the Chicago White Sox in the 37th round of the 2014 MLB Draft. Ed is an alumnus of St. Mary's High School in Stockton, California.

Edward Spragge

Edward Spragge (Peter Cross, ca. 1665)

Sir Edward Spragge (name also written as **Spragg** or **Sprague**) (circa 1620 - 11 August 1673) was an Irish admiral of the Royal Navy. He was a fiery, brilliantly accomplished seaman who fought in many great actions after the restoration of King Charles II in 1660.

Life

Spragge was son of Lichfield Spragge of Roscommon, Ireland, and grandson of an English settler. His father was killed in about 1645 during the Civil War when Royalist Governor of Roscommon.

Edward Spragge is said to have been a slave in Algiers before serving in the English Civil War from 1648 in Prince Rupert's royalist naval squadron. He remained loyal to the Stuarts after the war. When the royalist fleet had been dispersed in 1651, he began to work for the Dutch as a privateer in the First Anglo-Dutch War, which explains why some of his later colleagues had mixed feelings about him. He was very popular with the common sailors though because of his ebullient character; as

Samuel Pepys put it, "he was a merry man, singing a pleasant song pleasantly". After 1653, he became a pirate associating himself with the Flemish Collaert family, a group of Dunkirkers that after the French conquest of Dunkirk in 1646, had likewise been forced to seek employment elsewhere. Spragge married Clara, daughter of the famous privateer Jacob Collaert, the Governor of Dunkirk. He often clashed with Commonwealth vessels when employed by the Spanish as a privateer in the Anglo-Spanish War (1654).

After the English Restoration, Spragge was pardoned by Charles II and rewarded for his loyalty by being made captain of HMS *Drake*. Whenever Charles had need to send an envoy to the Spanish Netherlands, he often employed Spragge because of his good contacts there.

His first sea-fight with the Dutch was the Battle of Lowestoft in 1665, after which he was knighted on board of HMS *Royal Charles* for his gallant conduct as captain of the *Lion* (52), under Prince Rupert of the Rhine, who greatly favoured his career. Spragge was then given command of the *Triumph* (72). The next year he was rear-admiral of the Green Squadron, on the *Dreadnought* (58), under Prince Rupert and fought only in the fourth day of the Four Days Battle. He was vice-admiral of the Blue Squadron, subcommander of the rear, on the *Victory* (82), under Jeremiah Smith in the St. James's Day Battle. Although an overall English victory, the English rear was defeated and routed by Lieutenant-Admiral Cornelis Tromp. Spragge felt so humiliated by this course of events — also because he was publicly denounced as a coward for his conduct by his enemy Robert Holmes — that he became a personal enemy of Tromp, vowing to kill him. His attitude was also influenced by the rumour that Tromp had remarked that Spragge had in future better let his wife command his squadron, who no doubt were well qualified for it, given her background.

But Tromp was fired from the Dutch navy in August 1666. After the disaster of the Raid on the Medway, where Spragge was present, but unable to organize efficient resistance against the Dutch raiders, England had to conclude peace with the United Provinces and the Second Anglo-Dutch War came to an end. Spragge was thus satirized by Andrew Marvell for his failure to defend Sheerness fort:

Spragge there, though practised in the sea command,
With panting heart lay like a fish on land
And quickly judged the fort was not tenáble--
Which, if a house, yet were not tenantáble--
No man can sit there safe: the cannon pours
Thorough the walls untight and bullet showers,
The neighbourhood ill, and an unwholesome seat,
So at the first salute resolves retreat,
And swore that he would never more dwell there
Until the city put it in repair.
So he in front, his garrison in rear,
March straight to Chatham to increase the fear.

In 1670 and 1671, Vice Admiral Sir Edward Spragge fought the Barbary pirates on the *Revenge*. In the spring of 1671, he sailed with a fleet to Bougie Bay, near Algiers, where on 8 May, after a sharp fight, he burnt and destroyed ten corsair ships.

In 1672, the Third Anglo-Dutch War broke out, which gave Spragge the chance to deal with his old rival Tromp. At this time, Rupert and Spragge became rivals, the latter becoming jealous for not having been appointed supreme commander. Spragge was in command of the Red Squadron on the *London* in the Battle of Solebay in 1672 and of the Blue Squadron on the new *Prince Royal* of 100 cannon in the double Battle of Schooneveld of 1673. In these last Schooneveld battles he sought out and fought Tromp, readmitted to the navy in 1673, with great fury, but without result. Spragge publicly swore an oath in front of King Charles that the next time, he would either kill or capture his old enemy Tromp or die trying.

In the fourth Battle of Texel on 11 August 1673, Spragge and Tromp, commanding their respective rear divisions, again clashed repeatedly, each having their ships so damaged as to need to shift their flags to fresh ships twice. First the *Prince Royal* duelled the *Gulden Leeuw*; when the former ship was dismasted and half of her crew dead or wounded, Spragge shifted to HMS *St George* and Tromp to the *Comeetstar*. On the second occasion, whilst passing from the *St George* to the *Royal Charles*, Spragge's sloop was hit by cannon fire, a cannonball passing through the hull of the *St George* hitting the boat. The Admiral was injured but perhaps died by drowning as his vessel sank, just before reaching the ropes of the *St George* to which it had been rowed back as quickly as possible. The sloop remained partially floating and the body of Spragge was recovered with the head and shoulders still out of the water and his arms so cramped around the wood that much force had to be applied to free them. Contemporaneous Dutch naval historian Gerard Brandt wrote in his biography of Michiel de Ruyter: "This was the sad ending of Knight Edward Spragge, bravest of all English Admirals, who was praised by his friends and enemies for his courage and honesty and commiserated from compassion".

On 1 February 1673, Spragge had been elected as a Member of Parliament for Dover, after two ballots, but did not live to be able to sit. On 16 January 1674, it was resolved by Parliament that Spragge had failed to be elected because he had illegally influenced the election; he had in fact ordered an old and infirm pilot, who he knew intended to vote for his rival, aboard one of his ships, to prevent him from voting.

Spragge was buried in the North Choir Aisle of Westminster Abbey, but without any memorial visible today. His grave

had this inscription:
Sir Edward Spragge, Kt., a brave and valiant Sea Captain, who lost his life in a sea fight against the Hollanders, 1673

Namesakes

The Royal Navy has named four ships after Spragge. The first two, HMS *Spragge* of 1673 (renamed HMS *Young Spragge* in 1677) and HMS *Spragge* of 1677 were fireships. The third HMS *Spragge* was a destroyer leader cancelled in 1919. The fourth, HMS *Spragge* (K572), was a frigate in commission from 1944 to 1946 which saw service during World War II.

Elmer Sprague

Elmer Sprague is professor emeritus at Brooklyn College of the City University of New York, where he taught philosophy for 44 years. He has a B.A. from the University of Nebraska, and a B.A. and D.Phil. from Oxford. He was a Rhodes Scholar at Oxford (1948–51), and was the Paul Robert and Jean Shuman Hanna Professor of Philosophy at Hamline University (1987).

His previous publications include articles on Ryle and Hume, and the books, Metaphysical Thinking and What is Philosophy published by New York Oxford Press in 1961. His specialties are the philosophy of mind and philosophy of language. His book *Persons and their Minds*, published in 1999, is a Wittgensteinian-Ryleian critique of modern philosophy of mind.

The Lizardman

Erik Sprague (born June 12, 1972), better known as **The Lizardman**, is a freak show and sideshow performer, best known for his body modification, including his sharpened teeth, full-body tattoo of green scales, bifurcated tongue, subdermal implants and recently, green-inked lips.

The Lizardman makes his living as a freak, performing before audiences all over the world. He also makes numerous paid television and public appearances. He has mastered and regularly performs many classic sideshow acts such as the human blockhead, fire eating and breathing, gavage, sword swallowing, the bed of nails, the Human Dartboard, and the insectivore. He also participates in many public and private flesh hook suspension groups and events, and is highly involved in the body modification community. He also writes articles on the Body Modification E-zine. His rock band, LIZARD SKYNYRD, released an album in late 2010, they performed in many tours and stages across the world.

The Lizardman was born in Fort Campbell, KY, and was a Ph.D. candidate at the University at Albany before beginning his transformation. He holds a Bachelor of Arts degree in Philosophy from Hartwick College in Oneonta, New York.

The Lizardman lives in Austin, Texas.

Ernest Sprague

Born	October 20, 1865 Farmington, Michigan
Died	May 9, 1938 (aged 72) Cleveland, Ohio
Citizenship	United States
Alma mater	University of Michigan
Known for	Football player/Engineer

Ernest Marshall Sprague (October 20, 1865 - May 10, 1938) was an American football player, public official, and engineer. He was born in 1865 on a farm at Farmington, Michigan. He was the son of Lorenzo Sprague and Laura G. (Meade) Sprague. He enrolled at the University of Michigan where he played college football as a rusher for the 1886 Michigan Wolverines football team and as a left guard for the 1887 team. After graduating from Michigan in 1888, Sprague was an engineer with the Chicago & Northwestern Railway. He remained in that position until 1895. He next worked for the Milwaukee, Lake Shore & Western Railroad as a general inspector from approximately 1895 to 1897. His next position was with the Detroit Bridge & Iron Works. He moved to Denver, Colorado, as a representative of the Gillett Herzog Manufacturing Company in 1898. In 1900, he became employed with the American Bridge Company in Denver from 1900 to 1903. In 1903, he moved to Cleveland, Ohio where he continued to work for the American Bridge Company as a contracting engineer. As of 1915, he was the construction manager of the American Bridge Co. in Cleveland, Ohio. He moved to East Cleveland, Ohio in 1905 and was a member of that city's city council and a city commissioner for several years. He served on East Cleveland's City Commission from 1918 to 1934. He married Maude L. Sill in Colorado in 1902.

They had two children, Robert and Jean. At the time of the 1920 and 1930 U.S. Censuses, he lived in East Cleveland, Ohio, with his wife Maude. Sprague later worked for 18 years as a construction manager for Bethlehem Steel. He died in Cleveland at age 73 in 1938.

Frank J. Sprague

Frank Julian Sprague

Frank Julian Sprague (1857–1934) American inventor,
Father of Electric Traction

Born	July 25, 1857 Milford, Connecticut
Died	October 25, 1934 (aged 77)
Alma mater	United States Naval Academy
Known for	Electric motor
Notable awards	Elliott Cresson Medal (1903) IEEE Edison Medal (1910) Franklin Medal (1921) John Fritz Medal (Posthumous, 1935)

Frank Julian Sprague (July 25, 1857 in Milford, Connecticut - October 25, 1934) was an American naval officer and inventor who contributed to the development of the electric motor, electric railways, and electric elevators. His contributions were especially important in promoting urban development by increasing the size cities could reasonably attain (through better transportation) and by allowing greater concentration of business in commercial sections (through use of electric elevators in skyscrapers). He became known as the "Father of Electric Traction".

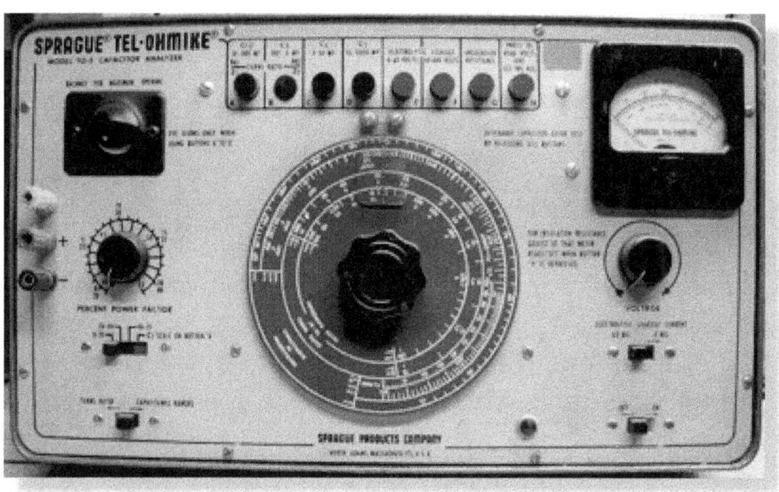

Early life and education

Sprague was born in Milford, Connecticut in 1857 to David Cummings Sprague and Frances Julia King Sprague. He attended Drury High School in North Adams, Massachusetts and excelled in mathematics. In 1874, he won an appointment to the United States Naval Academy in Annapolis, Maryland. There, he graduated seventh (out of thirty-six) in the Class of 1878.

US Navy, inventor

He was commissioned as an ensign in the US Navy. During his ensuing naval service, he first served on the USS *Richmond*, then the USS *Minnesota*. While his ship was in Newport, Rhode Island, in 1881, Sprague invented the inverted type of dynamo. After he was transferred to the USS *Lancaster*, flagship of the European Squadron, he installed the first electric call-bell system on a US Navy ship. Sprague took leave to attend the Paris Electrical Exhibition in 1881 and the Crystal Palace Exhibition in Sydenham, England in 1882, where he was on the jury of awards for gas engines, dynamos and lamps.

Electrical pioneer

In 1883, Edward H. Johnson, a business associate of Thomas Edison, persuaded Sprague to resign his naval commission to work for Edison. One of Sprague's significant contributions to the Edison Laboratory at Menlo Park, New Jersey, was the introduction of mathematical methods. Prior to his arrival, Edison conducted many costly trial-and-error experiments. Sprague's approach was to calculate using mathematics the optimum parameters and thus save much needless tinkering. He did important work for Edison, including correcting Edison's system of mains and feeders for central station distribution. In 1884, he decided his interests in the exploitation of electricity lay elsewhere, and he left Edison to found the Sprague Electric Railway & Motor Company.

By 1886, Sprague's company had introduced two important inventions: a constant-speed, non-sparking motor with fixed brushes, and regenerative braking, a method of braking that uses the drive motor to return power to the main supply system. His motor was the first to maintain constant speed under varying load. It was immediately popular, and was endorsed by Edison as the only practical electric motor available. His regenerative braking system was important in the development of the electric train and the electric elevator.

Electric streetcars

Postcard of electric trolley-powered streetcars in Richmond, Virginia, in 1923, two generations after Frank J. Sprague successfully demonstrated his new system onthe hills in 1888. The intersection shown is at 8th & Broad Streets.

Sprague's inventions included several improvements to designs for systems of electric streetcars collecting electricity from overhead wires. He improved designs for a spring-loaded trolley pole that had been developed in 1885 by Charles Van Depoele, devised a greatly improved mounting for streetcar motors and better gear designs, and proved that regenerative braking was practical. After testing his trolley system in late 1887 and early 1888, Sprague installed the first successful large electric street railway system – the Richmond

Union Passenger Railway in Richmond, Virginia, which began passenger operation on February 2, 1888. Long a transportation obstacle, the hills of Richmond included grades of over 10%, and were an excellent proving ground for acceptance of his new technology in other cities, in contrast to the cable cars which climbed the steepest grades of Nob Hill in San Francisco at the time.

By the summer of 1888, Henry H. Whitney of the West End Street Railway in Boston had witnessed the simultaneous startup of multiple streetcars on a single power source, and had signed up for conversion. By January 1889, Boston had its first electric streetcars, which were so popular and noteworthy that poet Oliver Wendell Holmes composed a verse about the new trolley pole technology, and the sparking contact shoe at its apex:

Since then on many a car you'll see
A broomstick as plain as plain can be;
On every stick there's a witch astride –
The string you see to her leg is tied.

Within a year, electric power had started to replace more costly horsecars in many cities. By 1889 110 electric railways incorporating Sprague's equipment had been begun or planned on several continents. In 1890, Edison, who manufactured most of Sprague's equipment, bought him out, and Sprague turned his attention to electric elevators.

Sprague's system of electric supply was a great advantage in relation to the first bipolar U-tube overhead lines, in everyday use since 1883 on Mödling and Hinterbrühl Tram.

Electric elevators

While electrifying the streetcars of Richmond, the increased passenger capacity and speed gave Sprague the notion that similar results could be achieved in vertical transportation: electric elevators. He saw that increasing the capacity of elevator shaft ways would not only save passengers' time, but would also increase the earnings of tall buildings, with height limited by the total floor space taken up in the shaft ways by slow hydraulic-powered elevators.

In 1892, Sprague founded the Sprague Electric Elevator Company, and with Charles R. Pratt developed the Sprague-Pratt Electric Elevator. The company developed floor control, automatic elevators, acceleration control of car safeties and a number of freight elevators. The Spague-Pratt elevator ran faster and with larger loads than hydraulic or steam elevators, and 584 elevators had been installed worldwide. Sprague then sold his company to the Otis Elevator Company in 1895.

Multiple unit train controls

Sprague's experience with elevator control led him to devise a multiple unit system of electric railway operation, which accelerated the development of electric traction. In the multiple unit system, each car of the train carries electric traction motors. By means of relays energized by train-line wires, the engineer (or motorman) commands all of the traction motors in the train to act together. For lighter trains there is no need for locomotives, so every car in the train can generate revenue. Where locomotives are used, one person can control all of them.

Sprague's first multiple unit order was from the South Side Elevated Railroad (the first of several elevated railways in locally known as the "L") in Chicago, Illinois. This success was quickly followed by substantial multiple-unit contracts in Brooklyn, New York and Boston, Massachusetts.

New York: Elevators in skyscrapers

From 1896 to 1900 Sprague served on the Commission for Terminal Electrification of the New York Central Railroad, including the Grand Central Terminal in New York City, where he designed a system of automatic train control to ensure compliance with trackside signals. He founded the Sprague Safety Control & Signal Corporation to develop and build this system. Along with William J. Wilgus, he designed the Wilgus-Sprague bottom contact third rail system used by the railroads leading into Grand Central Terminal.

During World War I, Sprague served on the Naval Consulting Board. Then, in the 1920s, he devised a method for safely running two independent elevators, local and express, in a single shaft, to conserve floor space. He sold this system, along with systems for activating elevator car safety systems when acceleration or speed became too great, to the Westinghouse Company.

Legacy and awards

The effect of Sprague's developments in electric traction was to permit an expansion in the size of cities, while his development of the elevator permitted greater concentration in cities' commercial sections and increased the profitability of commercial buildings. Sprague's inventions over 100 years ago made possible modern light rail and rapid transit systems which still function on the same principles today.
Sprague was awarded the gold medal at the Paris Electrical

Exhibition in 1889, the grand prize at the St. Louis Exhibition in 1904, the Elliott Cresson Medal in 1904, the Edison Medal of the American Institute of Electrical Engineers, now IEEE, in 1910 'For meritorious achievement in electrical science, engineering and arts as exemplified in his contributions thereto', the Franklin Medal in 1921 and the John Fritz Gold Medal (posthumously) in 1935.
"All through his life and up to his last day, Frank Sprague had a prodigious capacity for work", his son Robert wrote in 1935. "And once having made up his mind on a new invention or a new line of work, he was tireless and always striving for improvement. He had a brilliantly alert mind and was impatient of any half-way compromise. His interest in his work never ceased; only a few hours before the end, he asked to have a newly designed model of his latest invention brought to his bedside."

Frank and Harriet Sprague had two sons, Robert and Julian. Robert C. Sprague founded the Sprague Electric Company which became a leading manufacturer of capacitors and other electronic components. The company was later bought by Vishay in the 1990s.

After Sprague died in 1934, his widow Harriet turned over a substantial amount of material from his collection to the New York Public Library, where it remains today accessible to the public via the rare books division. He was buried at Arlington National Cemetery in Arlington, Virginia, and she was interred beside him after her death in 1969.

In 1959, Harriet Sprague had donated funds for the Sprague Building at the Shore Line Trolley Museum at East Haven, Connecticut, not far from Sprague's boyhood home in Milford. The museum is the oldest operating trolley museum in the United States, and has one of the largest collections of trolley artifacts in the United States.

In 1999, two of Frank and Harriet's grandsons, John L. Sprague and Peter Sprague, cut the ribbon and started an 1884 Sprague motor at a new exhibit at the Shore Line Trolley Museum. There, a permanent exhibit, "Frank J. Sprague: Inventor, Scientist, Engineer," helps tell the story of the part electricity played in the growth of cities as well as the role of the Father of Electric Traction. Entrepreneur Peter Sprague was Chairman of National Semiconductor from 1965 until 1995. John Sprague was President and Chief Executive Officer of Sprague Electric Company from 1981 to 1987.

Sprague's engines were used as far afield as Sydney Harbour, Australia. A five-horsepower Lundell electric motor used at the Cockatoo Island dockyard between 1900 and 1980 is now in the collection of the National Museum of Australia in Canberra.

In 2012, the Pennsylvania Trolley Museum adopted a stray cat, naming it after Sprague: Frank the Trolley Cat.

George Abel Sprague

Mayor of Dallas, Texas	
In office	
1937–1939	
Preceded by	George Sergeant
Succeeded by	Woodall Rodgers
Personal details	
Born	November 30, 1871 Preston, Fillmore County, Minnesota
Died	November 8, 1963 (aged 91) Dallas, Texas
Resting place	Oak Cliff Cemetery
Nationality	USA
Political party	Democrat
Spouse(s)	Minna Schwartz
Children	George S., Mortimer L., Elizabeth, Wilma, Howard Isaac, John F., Natalie, and Charles Cameron
Religion	Presbyterian

George Able Sprague (November 30, 1871 – November 8, 1963), businessman, was mayor of Dallas in 1935–1937.

George Able Sprague was born on November 30, 1871 in Preston, Fillmore County, Minnesota to Isaac Sprague and Anna Jeannette Plummer. He married Minna Schwartz, daughter of Ernest O. Schwartz and Elizabeth Gossman, on December 25, 1900 Preston, Fillmore, Minnesota. They had eight children: George S., Mortimer L., Elizabeth, Wilma, Howard Isaac, John F., Natalie, and Charles Cameron.

In Fillmore County, Minnesota, George Sprague taught school, operated a general store and was postmaster. As a traveling salesman, he came to Dallas where he eventually settled. He later managed a warehouse. He was active in the Oak Cliff area of Dallas and was active in the Oak Cliff Dads Club. He was involved in the formation of a Central Dads Club and headed it in its first year. His sons were noted for their skills in football at the collegiate level bringing recognition to Dallas.

He was elected to the city council in 1936 and 1937; and as mayor in 1937. In the 1937 city council election, George Sprague received the largest number of votes citywide. The city council then selected him as its mayor. During his time as mayor, Sprague supported the merger of Dallas, University Park and Highland Park and the election of the mayor by the citizens instead of the city council. The Dallas School Board named its new football stadium in southwest Dallas "Sprague Field" in honor of the family.

George Able Sprague died November 8, 1963 in Dallas, Texas and was interred at the Oak Cliff Cemetery, Dallas.

Franklin B. Sprague

Born	July 16, 1825 Delaware, Ohio
Died	February 7, 1895 (aged 69) Delaware, Ohio
Place of burial	Oak Grove Cemetery Delaware, Ohio
Service/branch	Union Army
Years of service	1864 - 1867
Rank	Captain
Unit	1st Oregon Volunteer Infantry
Commands held	I Company; Fort Klamath
Battles/wars	American Civil War Indian skirmishes
Other work	Businessman and judge

Franklin Burnet Sprague (July 16, 1825 – February 7, 1895) was an American military officer, businessman, and judge. He joined the Union Army during the Civil War, serving on the Oregon frontier. During his military service, Sprague explored much of Southern Oregon. While building a road near Fort Klamath, Sprague led a party into the Cascade Mountains to investigate Crater Lake. His party was the first to descend the 800-foot caldera wall to reach the lake's shore. A month later, Sprague published an article highlighting the lake's unique beauty. Today, the Sprague River in southern Oregon bears his name.

Early life

Sprague was born on July 16, 1825 in Delaware, Ohio. His parents were Pardon and Mary (Meeker) Sprague. His father was stockman, hotel keeper, county sheriff, and state legislator. Sprague received a private education in a small school near his home. He later attended Ohio Wesleyan University in his home town.

In 1850, Sprague moved to Oregon. He settled in Jackson County, where he opened a shop that built fanning-mills for winnowing grain. Sprague was the first manufacturer in the Pacific Northwest to produce modern winnowing machines. Like the majority of Oregonians at the time, Sprague was a strong supporter of the Union during the American Civil War.

Military service

In 1864, Sprague joined the Union Army, and was commissioned as a Captain in the 1st Oregon Volunteer Infantry Regiment. He was given command of I Company, and posted to Southern Oregon. He participated in a number of skirmishes with the Northern Paiute and other Indian bands in southeastern Oregon. In addition to fighting Indians, Sprague learned to speak their languages and counted many Indians among his friends, including the Modoc chief known as Captain Jack.

Captain Sprague was well respected as a leader, and often led detachments of cavalry as well as infantrymen. In October 1865, Sprague was leading a patrol of eleven cavalry troopers from C Company of the 1st Oregon Cavalry south of Warner Lake in present day Lake County, Oregon, when they were ambushed by approximately 125 Indians in two groups. Sprague and his troops were caught between a lake, high cliffs, and the two groups of Indians. After exchanging long-range gun fire with the Indians, Sprague determined that while the Indian in front of him had guns, those behind him had only bows and arrows. He quickly ordered his men to charge to the rear. His men broke through the Indian's skirmish line and made a successful escape with no casualties.

Crater Lake

Sprague and twenty men from Company I were assigned to build a road linking the Rogue River with the existing John Day road. This connected Jacksonville and southwest Oregon with John Day's mining country. After the construction work was completed, Sprague published a list of the best camp sites along the road in the Jacksonville newspapers so that the wagon masters could find the best water and grass along the way.

On August 1, 1865, two hunters from Sprague's road construction crew rediscovered Crater Lake, which had been first visited in 1853, but was never effectively recorded so that others could locate it. Based on directions from his hunters, Sprague and five other men visited the lake on August 12. They climbed down the 800-foot caldera cliff to become the first explorers to reach the lake shore. Sprague's account of the visit was reported to Jacksonville's leading newspaper, the *Oregon Sentinel* on August 25.

Wizard Island and Crater Lake's caldera

Sprague's report was published in the Oregon Sentinel on September 9, 1865. It included several significant observations. First, Sprague identified the volcanic origins of the lake. His report described Wizard Island, and observed it was a remnant of volcanic activity. Second, his description of the lake's unique beauty.

> *...you sit down on the brink of the precipice, and feast your eyes on the awful grandeur, your thoughts wander back thousands of years to the time when, where now is a placid sheet of water, there was a lake of fire, throwing its cinders and ashes to vast distances in every direction. The whole surroundings prove this lake to be the*

> *crater of an extinct volcano. The appearance of the water in the basin, as seen from the top of the mountain, is that of a vast circular sheet of canvass, upon which some painter had been exercising his art. The color of the water is blue, but in very many different shades, and like the colors in variegated silk, continually changing. Now a spot will be dark blue, almost approaching black, the next moment it will change to a very pale blue; and it is thus continually changing from one shade to another...*

Sprague also predicted that the lake would "be visited by thousands hereafter." Finally, he recommended that the lake not be named after its discoverer, saying: "I do not know who first saw this lake, nor do I think it should be named after the discoverer." Sprague suggested it be called "Lake Majestic." Today, it is known as Crater Lake. Since he was the first to identify the lake's volcanic origin, Sprague deserves some credit for the name.

Later life

On July 19, 1867, Captain Sprague and the men of Company I were mustered out of the Army. They were the last members of the 1st Oregon Volunteer Infantry Regiment to be released from active duty.[0]

In 1868, Sprague returned to Delaware County, Ohio. He

settled in Sunbury, where he started a grain milling business. In 1875, Sprague ran as the Democratic Party's candidate for Delaware County Probate Judge, and was elected. He was easily re-elected in 1878, completing his term in 1882. Sprague died on February 7, 1895. He is buried in the Oak Grove Cemetery in Delaware, Ohio.

Legacy

Sprague played an important part in the early history of Crater Lake National Park. His exploration party was the first to reach the lake's shore. He was the first to identify the lake's volcanic origin, and his article in the *Oregon Sentinel* generated public interest in Crater Lake's unique beauty.

In addition, Sprague explored much of Southern Oregon. The Sprague River is named after him. The Sprague River Valley, the town of Sprague River, and Sprague River Park in Fremont National Forest near Bly, Oregon also derive their names from Franklin Sprague.

Isaac Sprague

Isaac Sprague (September 5, 1811–1895) was a self-taught landscape, botanical, and ornithological painter. He was America's best known botanical illustrator of his day.

Sprague was born in Hingham, Massachusetts and apprenticed with his uncle as a carriage painter.

In 1843, Sprague assisted John James Audubon on an ornithological expedition up the Missouri River, taking measurements and making sketches. Young Sprague first met Audubon when the older man admired Sprague's bird drawings in 1840. His diary of this expedition is in the Boston Athenaeum.

Sprague's Pipit (*Anthus spragueii*), an uncommon and inconspicuous bird, was discovered on that expedition and named for Sprague. Some of Sprague's fine drawings were incorporated into Audubon's later publications.

In 1845 Sprague met Asa Gray (1810–1888) of Harvard College, and over many years illustrated several of his works including the plates for the atlas (1857) to Gray's "Botany. Phanerogamia" in Charles Wilkes' *United States Exploring Expedition During the Years 1838, 1839, 1840, 1841, 1842* (1845-1876). He also illustrated Asa Gray and John Torrey's various volumes of the U. S. War Departments Reports... *(1855–1860), as well as works for George B. Emerson, George Goodale, and Alpheus Baker Hervey.*

In 1960 Harvard University's Houghton Library exhibited approximately 100 of Sprague's paintings, drawings and illustrations. In 2003 Sprague's works were included in the Hunt Institute's exhibition *American Botanical Prints of Two*

Centuries.

Major collections of Sprague's work are held by the Boston Athenaeum, the Museum of Fine Arts (Boston), the Smithsonian Institution (on indefinite loan to the Hunt Institute for Botanical Verification, Carnegie Mellon University), and by Harvard University.

Isaac W. Sprague

Sprague in 1867, age 26

Isaac W. Sprague (May 21, 1841 - January 5, 1887) was an entertainer and sideshow performer, billed as the living human skeleton.

He was born on May 21, 1841, in East Bridgewater, Massachusetts. Although normal for most of his childhood, Sprague began losing weight at age 12 after feeling ill after swimming. In 1865, he joined a circus sideshow, becoming "the Living Skeleton" or "the Original Thin Man". The next year P. T. Barnum hired Sprague to work at his (newly reopened) American Museum until it burned down in 1868, continuing off and on to tour him throughout the country. By the age of 44, he was 5 feet and 6 inches tall with a weight of only 43 pounds.
He died on January 5, 1887, in poverty, of asphyxia in Chicago, Illinois.

He married Minnie Thompson and the couple had three strong, healthy, robust sons.

Ithamar Sprague

BY ED S - APRIL 17, 2012
POSTED IN: COLUMNS, OUR FAVORITE MORMONS

Doves & Serpents is initiating a new feature we call "Our Favorite Mormons." Consider it a biographical and uncorrelated version of Mormon.org, where we will tell the stories of Latter-day Saints, past and present, who have inspired us toward greater compassion, wonder or laughter. One of my favorite Mormons was Ithamar Sprague, a late 19th Century Latter-day Saint from southern Utah, a pioneer prankster who left big shoes for those of us who follow in his footsteps … literally. Also known as Mormonism's Other Bigfoot.

Bored by his life herding cattle near the Virgin River, Ithamar one day came across some smeared cow tracks in the mud resembling large footprints, inspiring him to make a very large pair of shoes and walk around town one night leaving enormous footprints in the dirt. The next day the town residents were all abuzz about the prints. Some wondered whether a monster, like Grendal, had been stalking them, awaiting the chance to tear them limb from limb and drink their sarsaparillas. Local Indian legends about a giant who had once prowled the countryside, laying waste to everything in his path, bolstered this view and panicked the locals. Others, more theologically-minded, suggested they were left by one of the 3 Nephites watching over them, or by Gadianton Robbers performing their secret combinations. How large feet, with shoes on, figured into identification of the footprints with these Book of Mormon characters was never elaborated upon. Sprague continued this prank for quite some time, all the while escaping detection in spite of the best efforts of his concerned neighbors.

How Sprague's prank was finally revealed is disputed in the variant tellings of this legend. My favorite version says that one night as the townspeople gathered to discuss the mysterious footprints, a girl noticed Sprague's hardly contained mirth and she asked him if he was behind it all. He then asked her what she would do if he admitted that he was the perpetrator. She whispered that if he confessed, then she would finally consent to marry him. In front of the crowd Sprague sprang up and admitted his guilt, much to the relief, then resentment, then (much later) affectionate laughter, of the crowd. They were then married and lived happily ever after.

John Russell Sprague

John Russell Sprague (December 24, 1886 - April 17, 1969) was the Republican county executive of Nassau County, New York from 1938 until 1953. He also was a delegate to the Republican National Convention in 1936, 1940, 1944, 1948, 1952, and 1956 and part of Republican National Convention from New York during 1940-1948.

Born in Inwood, New York, Sprague was an instrumental politician in Nassau County. He took center stage in adopting a county charter that created the position of county executive. In 1938, he was the first person elected to that office.

Jeffrey Russell Sprague

Jeffrey Russell Sprague (1965 –) is included here for the completely biased reason that he compiled this book! Jeff was born in San Jose, California, studied architecture at **Del Mar High School** and computer programming at various local colleges. He was a founding member of **PowerTV, Inc**., later acquired by **Scientific-Atlanta**, later acquired by **Cisco Systems**. He contributed tens of thousands of lines of code to the operating system of cable set-top-boxes and is currently the lead User Interface developer for Cisco's HTML-based video streaming application, known as Infinite Video. He has published a book of humor stories and essays, ***Slow Children At Play*** (available on Amazon) and has written *Thunder*, a screenplay about the building of the transcontinental railroad. Jeff won two awards from **General Motors** for producing the nation's best Corvette club newsletter for **Santa Clara Corvettes**. Obviously his design skills were not fully employed in the creation of this book. ☺

He married his high-school sweetheart almost 30 years ago and lives in Morgan Hill California, outside of San Jose, with a ginger dog, too many cats, and occasionally a son.

Jack Sprague

Jack Sprague (born August 8, 1964) is an American racing driver who has competed in all of NASCAR's three top divisions, but is most notable for his success in the Craftsman Truck Series (now Camping World Truck Series). Sprague has finished in the top-ten in the points standings almost every year he has raced in the trucks, and won three championships in 1997, 1999, and 2001 while driving for Hendrick Motorsports. He is currently a free agent, last driving for Wyler Racing.

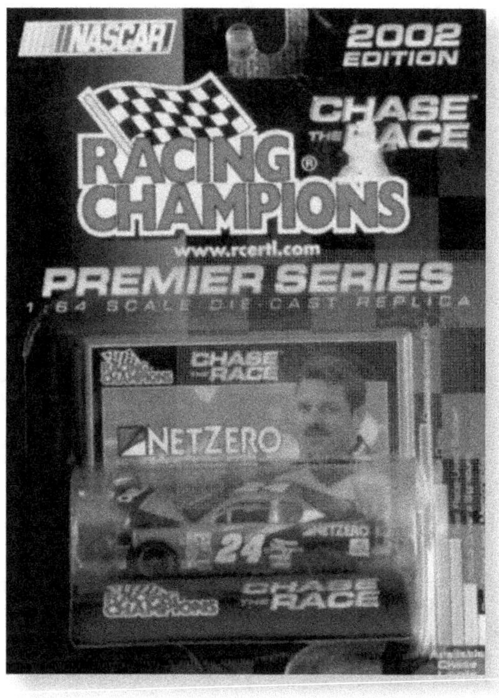

Racing career

Beginnings

Sprague was born in Spring Lake, Michigan, and began racing street stock cars at local short tracks. After winning the track championships at Thunderbird Raceway and later Winston Raceway, Sprague began racing in the NASCAR Winston Racing Series, in its North Carolina Late Model Division competition. He won the Big Ten Championship at Concord Motorsports Park, and won more than 30 Late Model Races. Eventually, he won the NASCAR Winston Racing Series championship at Concord Motorsports Park.

Sprague finished first in the inaugural race of the NASCAR Sportsman Division at Charlotte Motor Speedway in 1989, but was disqualified in post-race inspection, giving the win to Tim Bender.

Busch Series

Sprague made his Busch Series debut in 1989 at Charlotte Motor Speedway. Driving the #78 Griffin Racing Chevrolet, he qualified 28th but finished 41st after suffering engine failure early in the race. After a 40th-place finish at the Goody's 300 for Pucci & Associaties, Sprague moved up to drive the #34 Keystone Beer car for Frank Cicci Racing in 1990. He competed in nineteen races and had a best finish of sixth at Orange County Speedway. The following season, Sprague competed in seven races, driving the #48 Staff America Oldsmobile. He won his first career pole at Charlotte. He continued to drive the car in 1992, where he had a second-place finish at New River Valley Speedway. He finished 24th in the final standings.

In 1993, Sprague signed to drive the #74 BACE Motorsports car. Despite four top-ten finishes, he was released with just a handful of races left in the year. He finished nineteenth in points. Sprague returned to the Winston Cup Series in 1994.

Craftsman Truck Series

Sprague began racing in the Trucks' first year of competition in 1995. He began the season in the #31 Chevrolet Silverado for Griffin Racing, winning the pole at Louisville Speedway. After the Action Packed Racing Cards 150, Sprague switched to the #25 Budweiser Chevy for Hendrick Motorsports. He ended the season with a pole at Phoenix International Raceway, and had three fourth-place finishes.

In 1996, he slid over to the #24 Quaker State truck owned by Hendrick, winning his first race at Phoenix, followed up by back-to-back victories at Nazareth Speedway and The Milwaukee Mile. With five wins total and two poles, Sprague lost the championship by 53 points. That season, he made his Winston Cup debut, running a pair of races in the #52 Pedigree Petfoods Pontiac Grand Prix for Ken Schrader. He led two laps and finished 23rd in his debut at Phoenix, but wrecked the following week at Atlanta Motor Speedway.

The following season, Sprague won at Phoenix, Nazareth, and Nashville Speedway USA, and won the championship. In addition, he returned to the Cup series, subbing for Ricky Craven at Bristol Motor Speedway, but finished 40th after a wreck. Despite winning the Truck Series championship, Quaker State did not return as Sprague's primary sponsor, forcing him to start the 1998 unsponsored. After a one-race deal with Big Daddy's BBQ Sauce at Portland Speedway, Sprague won The No Fear Challenge in his debut for sponsor GMAC, allowing them to join full-time as sponsor. He won five races total that season and finished second in points. He returned to the Busch Series to drive the #40 Channellock Chevy for Doug Taylor at Watkins Glen International, finishing sixth. In 1999, Sprague won three races as well as the Craftsman Truck Series championship by eight points. He also drove at Watkins Glen in a Terry Labonte-owned car, finishing twelfth, and attempted the Exide NASCAR Select Batteries 400 for Tyler Jet Motorsports, but failed to qualify. He won three more times in 2000, but crashes caused him to drop to fifth in the standings. In 2001, NetZero became his primary sponsor, and he won seven poles and four races, and took home his third championship trophy.

Jo Ann Sprague

Member of the Massachusetts Senate from the Bristol and Norfolk district	
In office	
2003–2004	
Member of the Massachusetts Senate from the Norfolk, Bristol, and Plymouth district	
In office	
1999–2002	
Member of the Massachusetts House of Representatives from the 9th Norfolk district	
In office	
1993–1999	
Personal details	
Born	November 3, 1931 Nashville, Tennessee
Political party	Republican
Residence	Walpole, Massachusetts
Occupation	Legislator

Jo Ann Sprague (born November 3, 1931) is a former Massachusetts State Representative (1993–1998) and State Senator (1999–2004) from Walpole. In the Massachusetts Senate she represented the Norfolk, Bristol, and Plymouth district, but moved in 2003 to the Bristol and Norfolk district. Previously she was a State Representative from the 9th Norfolk district. She is a member of the Republican Party.

Sprague was born in Nashville, Tennessee. She graduated from the University of Massachusetts Boston in 1980 with a B.A. in classical studies. She served as a selectman in Walpole, Massachusetts from 1977 to 1980, a member of the Walpole

Capital Budget committee from 1980 to 1992, a member of the Walpole Republican Town Committee. She was elected to the Massachusetts House of Representatives and served from 1993 to 1998, then served in the Massachusetts Senate from 1999 to 2004. She ran for the United States House of Representatives in 2001 to represent Massachusetts's 9th congressional district, but lost to Democratic opponent Stephen Lynch.

John W. Sprague

John Wilson Sprague	
Brigadier General John W. Sprague	
Born	April 4, 1817 White Creek, New York
Died	December 27, 1894 (aged 77) Tacoma, Washington
Place of burial	Tacoma Cemetery
Allegiance	United States of America Union
Service/branch	Union Army
Years of	1861–1866

service	
Rank	Brigadier General Brevet Major General
Unit	Army of the Tennessee
Commands held	63rd Ohio Infantry 2nd Brigade, 4th Division, XVI Corps
Battles/wars	American Civil War Battle of New Madrid Battle of Island Number Ten Siege of Corinth Battle of Iuka Vicksburg Campaign Atlanta Campaign Sherman's March to the Sea Carolinas Campaign
Awards	Medal of Honor
Other work	Businessman, county treasurer, railroad executive

John Wilson Sprague (April 4, 1817 - December 27, 1894) was an American soldier and railroad executive. He served as a general in the Union Army in the Western Theater of operations during the American Civil War. He received the Medal of Honor for gallantry at the Battle of Decatur during the Atlanta Campaign. After the war, he was a railroad executive and later co-founded the city of Tacoma, Washington, serving as its first mayor.

Early life and career

John W. Sprague was born in White Creek, New York, on April 4, 1817, the son of Otis and Polly (Peck) Sprague. He was educated in the district school of his neighborhood and at the age of thirteen entered the Rensselaer Polytechnic Institute at Troy, New York. He left school before graduation to engage in the grocery business, and in 1845 removed to Milan, Ohio, where he continued the business of a merchant in the shipping and commission sales businesses. He afterward settled in Sandusky and was for one term (1851–52) the treasurer of Erie County, Ohio.

He was married to Lucy Wright, daughter of a judge of Huron County, Ohio. However, she died in Troy, New York, in May 1844, not long after giving birth to a daughter. He was remarried to Julia Frances Choate of Milan; the couple had five children of their own.

In the late 1850s he organized and equipped a line of sailboats and steamers for traffic on Lake Erie and was engaged in that business when war erupted.

Civil War service

With the outbreak of the Civil War and President Abraham Lincoln's call for 100,000 volunteers to put down the rebellion, Sprague raised a company of infantry and was sent to Camp Dennison near Cincinnati. Upon being mustered into Federal service, he became the captain of Company E of the 7th Ohio Infantry. While returning home on furlough in August 1861, he and a small party of fellow Buckeyes were captured in West Virginia and held as prisoners of war. Sprague was exchanged in January 1862 and returned to his regiment.

Later that month, Sprague was appointed as the colonel of the newly designated 63rd Ohio Infantry, The regiment was organized on January 23 by consolidating partially filled battalions from the 22nd Ohio Infantry and the 63rd Ohio regiments. After brief training and drilling, Sprague and his men took the field, traveled via train to the South, and joined Major General John Pope in Missouri. Sprague led the regiment at the Siege of Corinth, Mississippi, and then was in charge of the Ohio Brigade during the Battle of Iuka in 1862.

For the next several months, Sprague took part in the army's general operations in northern Alabama and Mississippi, extending sometimes into Tennessee. He participated in the Vicksburg Campaign in early and mid-1863. In the fall of 1863, as part of the forces under Maj. Gen. William T. Sherman, he moved with his regiment eastward toward Chattanooga, Tennessee. He regiment was part of the force under command of General Grenville M. Dodge that was detached to secure the railroad to Decatur, Alabama.

During the 1864 Atlanta Campaign, Sprague was in command of the 2nd Brigade, 4th Division of the Sixteenth Army Corps. During the Battle of Atlanta on July 22, 1864, at a subaction near Decatur, Georgia, he masterfully conducted a delaying action under heavy enemy fire and received praise from his superiors. With only a small command, he defeated an overwhelming Confederate force and saved the entire ordnance and supply trains of the XV, XVI, XVII, and XX corps.

Sprague was promoted to the rank of brigadier general on July 30, 1864. He moved with Sherman on the March to the Sea and then northward during the Carolinas Campaign. He commanded the brigade on its march from Raleigh, North Carolina, through Richmond to Washington, D.C., and participated in the Grand Review of the Armies in May. At the end of the war, he received the brevet rank of major general.

From April 1865 until September 1866, Sprague was the assistant commissioner of the Freedmen's Bureau for the district of Arkansas, serving under Maj. Gen. Oliver O. Howard. He was in charge of operations in Missouri, Kansas, and subsequently the Indian Territory. In September 1865, he declined a lieutenant-colonelcy in the Regular Army and mustered out of the service. He was succeeded by Edward O. C. Ord.

Postbellum career

He was appointed as the manager of the Winona & St. Paul Railway in Minnesota. In 1870 he became the general manager of the Western Division of the Northern Pacific Railway and co-established the city of Tacoma, Washington, on Puget Sound. He was instrumental in selecting the route for the railroad's Pacific Division, from what later became Kalama, Washington, to Tacoma. In 1883 he had the honor of driving the golden spike on the completion of his division. However, he suffered from poor health and was forced to resign a few months later.

He was active in building up the new city of Tacoma and was president of the board of trade and of various banks and corporations. He served as the town's first mayor, became prominent in its financial circles, and was president of the National Bank, Tacoma Chamber of Commerce, and the Tacoma Steam Navigation Company. His second wife Julia died in 1886. He later married Abigail Choate.

The town of Sprague, Washington, founded in 1880, was named for General Sprague. Lincoln County, Washington, was originally named for Sprague, until opposition from

political enemy (and former Union colonel) Joseph H. Houghton, a Washington Territory legislator.
After suffering for several years from heart disease and chronic cystitis, Sprague died at his home in Tacoma on December 27, 1893, and was buried in the city's cemetery. In 1894 the United States Congress awarded the Medal of Honor to General John W. Sprague for distinguished gallantry during the Battle of Decatur. However, Sprague never saw his medal, having died several weeks before it arrived.

The John W. Sprague Camp of the Sons of Union Veterans of the Civil War was named in his honor.

Medal of Honor citation

Rank and Organization: Colonel, 63d Ohio Infantry. Place and Date: At Decatur, Ga., 22 July 1862. Entered Service At: Sandusky, Ohio Born: 4 April 1817, White Creek, N.Y. Date of Issue: 18 January 1894.

Citation:
With a small command defeated an overwhelming force of the enemy and saved the trains of the corps.

Kate Chase Sprague

(Book and description from Amazon.com)

The charismatic daughter of Salmon P. Chase, Lincoln's treasury secretary, Kate Chase enjoyed unprecedented political power for a woman. As her widowed father's hostess, she set up a rival "court" against Mary Lincoln in hopes of making her father president and herself his First Lady. To facilitate that goal, she married one of the richest men in the country, the handsome "boy governor" of Rhode Island, in the social event of the Civil War. She moved easily between the worlds of high fashion, adorning herself in the most regal Parisian gowns, and politics, managing her father's presidential campaigns. "No Queen has ever reigned under the Stars and Stripes," one newspaper would write, "but this remarkable woman came closer to being a Queen than any American woman has."

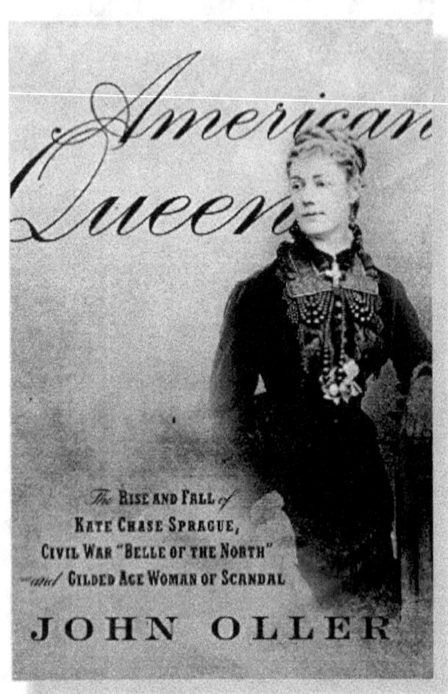

But when William Sprague turned out to be less of a prince as a husband, Kate found comfort in the arms of a powerful married senator. The ensuing sex scandal ended her virtual royalty; after the marriage crumbled and the money disappeared, she was left only with her children and her ever-proud bearing. She became a social outcast and died in poverty, yet in her final years she would find both greater authenticity and the inner peace that had always eluded her.

From mrlincolnswhitehouse.org:

Daughter of Secretary of the Treasury Salmon P. Chase, Kate Chase Sprague married Rhode Island Senator William Sprague during the Civil War. She was beautiful, charming, precocious, a leading social figure in Washington at 19, and a top political aide to her father until his death.

Salmon P. Chase had little luck building a family. Three wives died and four of their six children died as well. Kate Chase, the oldest surviving daughter, was spoiled and ambitious. She had been packed off to boarding school at age 9 because she didn't get along with her stepmother. At 21, she set out to be the First Lady of Washington in fact if not name. She had no intention of acquiring another stepmother – despite her father's interest in women such as Adele Cutts Douglas, the widow of Senator Stephen Douglas.

Despite her youth, Kate Chase was the reigning social queen of Washington during the Civil War. Biographer Peg A. Lamphier wrote: "After Willie Lincoln's death from typhoid fever in early 1862, the mourning Mrs. Lincoln may have remained the titular head of Washington society, but Kate reigned as its sovereign queen."[2] Historian Doris Kearns Goodwin wrote: "Her social supremacy derived in part from her striking appearance, enhanced by the simple but elegant wardrobe assembled during her many trips to New York in pursuit of furnishings for her father's mansion."[3]

Kate had an enchanting effect on men. Historian Doris Kearns Goodwin wrote: "Kate's dynamic grace and intellect made her the most interesting woman in any gathering, as well as a critical force behind her father's drive for the presidency."[7] She wrote that Kate's "father's ambitions and reams became the ruling passions of her life. She gradually made herself absolutely essential to him, helping with his correspondence, editing his speeches, discussing political strategy, entertaining his friends and colleagues. While other girls her age focused on the social calendar of balls and soirées, she concentrated all her energies on furthering her father's political career."[8]

Kate's extravagance in clothes, however, threatened her father's fragile budget. Her expensive shopping habits were an attribute she shared with the First Lady with whom she shared little else. Kate maintained that her relationship with Mary Todd Lincoln was doomed when she failed to attend a reception in Columbus with her in 1859. "Mrs. Lincoln was piqued that I did not remain at Columbus to see her, and I have always felt that this was the chief reason why she did not like me at Washington."[9]

Like much of male Washington, Rhode Island Senator William Sprague was clearly infatuated with Kate. He admitted: "The business which takes my time, my attention, my heart, my all...is of a certain young lady who has become so entwined in every pulsation, that my former self has lost its identity."

President Lincoln attended the opulent Chase-Sprague wedding in November 1863. Mrs. Lincoln was conspicuously absent. Chase family chronicler Lamphier wrote: "By 7:30 on the evening of 12 November, carriages lined both Sixth and E. Streets to deliver their passengers at Salmon P. Chase's rented Greek Revival mansion. Traffic came to a veritable standstill for blocks while elite Washington society waited to gain entrance to the social event of the season."[13] Presidential aide William O. Stoddard wrote: "The social event of the past week was the wedding of Senator Sprague and Miss Chase. Never did anything go off more neatly. The 'tableau,' as they call it, at the marriage itself was charming; and the dress reception in the evening, and the informal one next day, were entirely pleasant. The presents were magnificent - silver, pearls, diamonds, &c., to the tune of a hundred thousand or so.

Ken Sprague

Ken Sprague (1927-2004) was an English socialist political cartoonist, journalist and activist, involved in trade union, civil rights and peace movements. In later life he was also a TV presenter and a psychotherapist.
Sprague was concerned with how politics affected the ordinary person. "In essence, the leitmotif of his work is about power and the abuse of power as well as the resilience of ordinary working people to this abuse... It is an art of engagement - engagement for change." Martin Rowson said "Ken's art has the power and strength to inspire. He is the true heir, as a socialist artist, of William Morris."

Early years

Sprague was born in Bournemouth, to a father who was a train driver and a mother who worked in a cardboard box factory. His first work of art, in 1937, in response to the Guernica air raid in the Spanish Civil War, was a linocut made from linoleum torn from the kitchen floor. Printed on his mother's mangle, it was used on collecting sheets for Spain.

He was educated at Alma Road Elementary School — until it

was bombed during World War II – and Porchester Road Secondary Modern School. There the headmaster, noticing his talent, recommended that he apply to the local art college. He won a scholarship to Bournemouth Municipal College and, from 13 and a half, studied graphics – since in those days students of his background were rarely considered for fine arts courses.

One morning in 1944 he volunteered for the Royal Marines, aged 17, – and that same afternoon, in Southampton, he joined the Communist Party. After basic military training he was transferred to Vickers-Supermarine as a technical artist, working on ejector seats for Spitfires. He was also sent to Yugoslavia to bring back an ejector seat from a German plane the partisans had shot down, during which visit he adopted the big handlebar moustache that was to become his trademark for the rest of his life.

Postwar, and after a summer stint in a circus, he completed his college diploma course in design and illustration. The Communist Party, he told his biographer, was his university, but after the *Bournemouth Daily Echo* had labelled him a college revolutionary, local job prospects dwindled. He briefly worked for a volunteer labour battalion in Yugoslavia, and was employed by the Boy Scouts.

Activist journalist/artist

Between 1950 and 1954 Sprague worked in a Carlisle mining company design office – doubling as a cartoonist for the local Conservative and Liberal newspapers. Then came a move to London as the *Daily Worker*'s publicity manager, which also had him working as a journalist and cartoonist. Devastated by the Soviet invasion of Hungary in 1956, in 1959 Sprague left to set up, with Ray Barnard, the publicity company, Mountain &

Molehill (M&M). Yet he continued producing cartoons for the *Worker*, and its successor the *Morning Star*, into the 21st century.

M&M – later The Working Arts – was responsible for some of the most innovative trade union campaigns of the 1960s and 1970s. Sprague told union leaders they had to use publicity to win hearts and minds and to see it as an integral part of union work. And it was Sprague and Barnard who initiated the sensational 1961 visit to Britain of the first man in space, Soviet cosmonaut Yuri Gagarin, inviting the former foundry worker to speak to the Amalgamated Union of Foundry Workers (now part of Amicus). M&M also worked for the Indian High Commission, which led to a meeting with Jawaharlal Nehru.

During the 1950s and '60s, Sprague also did several set designs for the left-wing Unity Theatre, including productions of George Bernard Shaw's *The Apple Cart*, Anton Chekhov's *The Cherry Orchard* and Arthur Miller's *The Crucible*.

In the late 1960s Ken began editing the Transport and General Workers' Union's *The Record*, transforming it into a lively newspaper, and illustrating it with his own cartoons. In 1976 he edited the anti-fascist magazine *Searchlight* for some months, before being sacked when he published a criticism of Israeli oppression of Palestinians.
As a poster and print-maker he worked with a number of leading progressive organisations and individuals, including Pete Seeger. He drew political cartoons for the *Daily Worker* and its successor the *Morning Star*, and for *Tribune* and *Peace News*. He created posters for among others Martin Luther King and the Greenham Common Women's Peace Camp. He created posters against Edward Heath's Industrial Relations Act 1971 and the 1984 miners' strike, but among his most powerful works are those relating to war, including the Soviet

invasion of Czechoslovakia, the Iran–Iraq War, and the Kosovo war. He was a war artist during the Iran–Iraq War, accompanying an Iraqi regiment during an attack on the oil town of Abadan when it lost 582 men in a single day. He met Saddam Hussein and sketched him. He encountered some criticism form comrades, given Hussein's brutal dictatorship (including CIA-supported slaughter of communists), but Sprague maintained he was documenting the horrors of war, the subject which had first brought him to political art. He won several prestigious awards, including poster of the year award from the Council of Industrial Design on two occasions.

His linocuts for the radical collective Cinema Action's *Kill The Bill* film (1971), relating to the Industrial Relations Bill, began an involvement in moving images, which led to Jeff Perks's 1976 BBC Omnibus documentary *The Posterman*. This led to a series of Channel 4 films, devised with Jeff Perks and presented by Ken, called *Everyone A Special Kind Of Artist* (1986). There was also a 1979 BBC South West series *The Moving Line*, with Joan Bakewell.

Later life

In 1971 he moved with his wife, Sheila, a talented potter, to Holwell, a farmhouse in Devon, and converted it into an artistic centre. Sheila died of cancer in 1973, but with his second wife, Marcia, he set up the Holwell International Centre for Psychodrama and Sociodrama which continued until 1998. There Ken combined his artistic talents with pedagogic expertise, using them in this new field in which he became a leading practitioner. The project hit difficulties shortly after an unexpected demand for a large VAT payment by HM Revenue and Customs. Ken and Marcia moved to a smaller house, Hoewell, in Lynton, where they continued the

work begun in Holwell.
Sprague left the Communist Party after its acrimonious split in 1988. He continued to call himself a communist, however, saying "The party left me, I didn't leave the party".

Lucian Sprague

Lucian C. Sprague (1882–1960) was an American railroad executive. Sprague was born in Serena, Illinois, on September 29, 1882, and during his early years held a variety of railroad jobs, including stints at the Chicago, Burlington and Quincy, Great Northern, and Baltimore and Ohio. In 1922, he was hired by the Uintah Railway, a remarkable and remote narrow gauge short line in the mountains along the Colorado-Utah border. Sprague remained at the Uintah for most of the decade, becoming the line's general manager.

In 1935, Sprague was appointed co-receiver of the bankrupt Minneapolis and St. Louis Railway (M&StL), a mid-sized railroad that extended south and west from Minneapolis. The M&StL had struggled financially for years, and by the 1930s was threatened with liquidation; Sprague, however, managed to turn the company around, and the railroad's twenty-year receivership ended in 1943. Sprague was named president of the M&StL at the end of receivership, and he held that position until being ousted in a dramatic 1954 shareholders battle orchestrated by Benjamin W. Heineman.

Sprague died of a heart attack in Minneapolis in 1960.

Sprague Grayden

The actress's Twitter bio reads: "actress, geek, all around nerd." She's a self-proclaimed sci-fi geek (especially when it comes to Battlestar Galactica), Doctor Who, and X-Men. She played First Daughter Olivia Taylor in **24**, Anita Miller in **Six Feet Under**, Judith Montgomery in **Joan of Arcadia**, Heather Lisinski in **Jericho**, Donna Winston in **Sons of Anarchy**, and had a guest appearance on **Weeds**.

She might not qualify based on Sprague being her first name, but she does, in fact, have the lineage. Sprague is her mother's maiden name. She was born in Manchester, Massachusetts on July 21, 1980.

Peleg Sprague (Maine politician)

Member of the U.S. House of Representatives
from Maine's 4th district
In office
March 4, 1825 – March 3, 1829
United States Senator
from Maine
In office

March 4, 1829 – January 1, 1835	
Personal details	
Born	April 27, 1793 Duxbury, Massachusetts
Died	October 13, 1880 (aged 87) Boston, Massachusetts
Political party	National Republican
Alma mater	Harvard University

Peleg Sprague (April 27, 1793 - October 13, 1880) was an American politician from the U.S. state of Maine, and a United States federal judge.

Born in Duxbury, Massachusetts, Sprague graduated from Harvard University in 1812, and studied law at the Litchfield Law School in Litchfield, Connecticut. He was admitted to the bar in August 1815 and began practice in Augusta, Maine. In 1817, he moved to Hallowell, where he continued his practice.

Sprague's political career began when he served as a member of the Maine House of Representatives from 1821 to 1822. In 1823, he was elected to the U.S. House of Representatives from Maine's fourth congressional district, serving from March 4, 1825, to March 3, 1829, when he became a member of the United States Senate. Sprague continued to serve in the Senate until January 1, 1835, when he again resigned. During his time in the Senate Sprague became a prominent campaigner against President Andrew Jackson's controversial policy of Indian removal, whereby Indians in the Southern states were to be forcibly relocated to West of the Mississippi River. Sprague argued that the policy was corrupt as it largely relied on bribes for support, and he also attacked the plan for its immorality and lack of humanity, claiming that the Indians would receive no assistance in starting new lives in an alien environment. After resigning from the Senate in 1835, Sprague practiced law in Boston from 1836 to 1841. He was a presidential elector on the Whig ticket in 1840.

On July 15, 1841, Sprague was nominated by President John Tyler to a seat on the United States District Court for the District of Massachusetts vacated by John Davis. Sprague was confirmed by the United States Senate on July 16, 1841, and received his commission the same day. Sprague's service was terminated on March 13, 1865, due to resignation.

Sprague died in Boston in 1880. He is buried in the Mount Auburn Cemetery in Cambridge. Sprague was a corporate member of the Maine Historical Society.

Peleg Sprague (New Hampshire politician)

Member of the U.S. House of Representatives from New Hampshire's At-large district (Seat 1)	
In office	
December 15, 1797 - March 3, 1799	
Personal details	
Born	December 10, 1756 Rochester, Province of Massachusetts Bay
Died	April 20, 1800 (aged 43) Keene, New Hampshire
Political party	Federalist
Residence	Keene
Alma mater	Harvard University, Dartmouth College
Profession	Attorney

Peleg Sprague (December 10, 1756 - April 20, 1800) was a politician from the U.S. state of New Hampshire.

Sprague was born in Rochester, Massachusetts. He clerked in a store in Littleton, Massachusetts, attended Harvard College, and was graduated from Dartmouth College, Hanover, New Hampshire, in 1783. He studied law, was admitted to the bar in 1785, and commenced practice in Winchendon, Massachusetts. He moved to Keene, New Hampshire, in 1787. He was selectman 1789-1791; county solicitor for Cheshire County in 1794; and member of the New Hampshire House of Representatives in 1797.

Sprague was elected as a Federalist Party to the 5th United States Congress to fill the vacancy caused by the resignation of Jeremiah Smith, serving from December 15, 1797, to March 3, 1799. He declined to be a candidate for renomination in 1798.

Sprague died in Keene, New Hampshire, and was interred there in the Washington Street Cemetery.

Peter Sprague

Background information	
Birth name	Peter Tripp Sprague
Born	October 11, 1955 (age 59) Cleveland, Ohio, United States
Genres	Jazz, jazz fusion, folk jazz, world fusion, post-bop, jazz-rock, crossover jazz
Occupation(s)	Musician, composer, audio engineer, record producer
Instruments	Acoustic guitar, electric guitar, guitar synthesizer
Years active	1976–present
Labels	Concord Records, Xanadu Records, SBE Records
Associated acts	Blurring the Edges, Dance of the Universe, David Benoit, Chick Corea and Friends, Dianne Reeves, Geoffrey Keezer/Peter Sprague Group, Peter Sprague String Consort, Peter Sprague Trio, Sergio Mendes and Brasil '99
Website	petersprague.com
Notable instruments	
Twin-neck guitar with one neck nylon string, the other neck steel string	

Peter Sprague (Peter Tripp Sprague, born October 11, 1955) is a critically acclaimed American jazz guitarist, composer, musical arranger and musical transcriber, sound recording engineer, and music producer. In 1984 noted jazz critic Leonard Feather, in a review for the *Los Angeles Times*, called

Sprague, "One of the emergent great guitarists." While he is highly conversant with many forms of both jazz and classical music, his own compositions and arrangements have often reflected a Latin flavor, though lately he has created and performed a number of pieces specifically for his "String Consort" group (featuring a string quartet of violins, viola, and cello) which range from classical- to American folk-originated explorations. He owns and operates SpragueLand Studios where he is studio recording engineer and often plays as one of the performing musicians. He also owns and has been producing for his own record label, SBE Records, since 1994. Although he lives in the North County region of San Diego, California and performs frequently in the San Diego and greater Southern California region, he has traveled to and performed in a number of international venues. He has one brother, jazz saxophonist Tripp Sprague, and one sister, Dr. Terry Sprague (PhD), who teaches dance as depicted on film and video. He is married to Stefanie Flory, an Occupational Therapist and the manager of SpragueLand Studios. They have one daughter, Kylie Sprague, born in 1993, and live in Leucadia, California.

Richard E. Sprague

Richard E. Sprague was an American computer technician, researcher and author. According to American journalist Dick Russell, who dedicated seventeen years to the investigation of John Kennedy assassination, Sprague was "the leading gatherer of photographic evidence about the Kennedy assassination". Sprague published his investigation in 1985 as *The Taking of America.*

Robert C. Sprague

Founder of Sprague Electric

Robert C. Sprague	
Born	August 2, 1900 New York City, New York
Died	September 27, 1991 (aged 91) Williamstown, Massachusetts
Nationality	American

Robert C. Sprague (August 2, 1900 - September 27, 1991) was the son of Frank J. Sprague Jr and Harriet Sprague. Sprague founded Sprague Electric (originally Sprague Specialties Company), Quincy, MA in 1926, and served as president from 1926-1953 and chief executive from 1953-1971. He invented the tone control for radio and the paper capacitor that launched his business.

Sprague was appointed by President Eisenhower to serve as Undersecretary to the Air Force in 1953. He accepted then rejected the position due to financial difficulties.

Sprague Electric was an electronic component maker and was best known for making a large line of capacitors (electron storage device) used in a wide variety of electrical and electronic in commercial, industrial and military/space applications. Other products include resistive components, magnetic components (transformers and coils), filter assemblies, semiconductors and integrated circuits. Sprague had one brother, Julian Sprague, who assisted in company operations. Sprague capacitor products were bought and absorbed by Vishay in the early 1993.

Education and Adulthood

After graduating from The Hotchkiss School in 1918, Robert Sprague followed his father Frank's (a business associate to Thomas Alva Edison) footsteps, and went to the United States Naval Academy in Annapolis. He later attended the Naval Post Graduate School and completed his graduate program at the Massachusetts Institute of Technology (MIT). While a naval officer he invented the tone control for amplifiers and radio sets. In 1921 he married Florence Antoinette van Zelm. They were married until her death in 1987. Sprague patented the paper condenser (capacitor) and tone control in 1926, and this provided the capitol to start a business.

Sprague Specialties Company (1926-1942)

Sprague used $25,000 of his savings to open Sprague Specialties Company at his home in Quincy, MA, in 1926. One of his first products was the mini condenser (an old name for capacitor). Mini condensers were commonly used in radio applications for noise filtering, signal coupling and tone controls. Early capacitors were two pieces of metal foil wrapped between wax paper or any other type of suitable insulation material. The type of insulating material determined the capacitor's storage capacity (measured in

Farads) and the voltage tolerated. Wire leads from the capacitor connect to each metal foil. Capacitors were also useful in high power applications like motors, and soon Sprague turned his attention those areas as well.

Sprague found a sustainable product line in capacitors. The increase in the types of radios using AC created demand for many different types of capacitors. By 1929 Sprague Specialties Company needed a bigger facility, and in 1930 Sprague purchased a plant on Beaver Street in North Adams, MA, in Berkshire County. When local residents heard the company was expanding, Sprague received all kinds of incentives from the banks and other businesses to relocate there. Sprague chose the area because he wanted to open a shop where his father Frank had grown up.

By the mid-1930s Sprague had become a recommended source for capacitors by radio manufacturers, radio repair and many electrical applications. As the size of the company grew there was a desire from the manufacturing workers to form an organized labor union. The Wagner Act of 1935 prohibited company unions. In 1937 the company agreed with the workers to form an independent union, the Independent Condenser Workers Union.

From 1936-1944, the Sprague Specialties Company sales increased seven-fold, however expansion put a damper to profits. For many years the company sustained losses. Robert felt strongly connected to his company and to the people of North Adams, and always tried to put the town population first. As a result, the Sprague Specialties Company became the largest employer in North Adams.

By 1942 the Sprague Specialties Company relocated to the abandoned Arnold Print Works Facility on Marshall St. This became the main facility and consisted of 26 buildings that were interconnected by tunnels and bridges. Former employees remember the complex layout and interesting ways to get from one department to another. Previous to the Sprague Specialties Company, the Arnold Print Works had been the largest employer in North Adams, operating in the area from 1860-1942.

Also in 1942 company's name changed from Sprague Specialty Products to Sprague Electric. The Sprague Electric name would remain until its last owner Penn Central started to sell off the Sprague division in the early 1990s.

The Sprague Log (1938-1985)

Beginning in 1938 Sprague tried to bridge the gap between the people and the business with the publication of the *Sprague Log*. Sprague used this newsletter to bring management and workers closer, and to maintain morale after forcing workers to take a 10% pay cut that same year. The publication was divided into two sections. Part 1 discusses the company accomplishments, achievements and the loyalty of Sprague employees, often spotlighting individuals. Part 2 are employee announcements - births and weddings, social activities and other family events.

Sprague Electric: Early years (1942-1960)

After the Japanese invasion of Pearl Harbor on December 7, 1941 and the declaration of war that followed, US manufacturing stopped commercial production and switched to wartime activities. Sprague Electric's participation in the US war effort proved to be a healthy one in reputation, future contracts, and sales, and propelled the Sprague name to the forefront of the American electronic business.

One of Sprague Electric's biggest contributions to the war effort was in the manufacturing of the variable timing proximity fuze. The proximity fuse was a small transmitter (and in some cases a receiver) built on a bomb or artillery shell that would detonate the bomb or shell before impact, causing greater destruction. Sprague Electric continued to make capacitor and resistive components to meet military requirements of quality and reliability. Robert C. Sprague was also a member of War Production Board for the Advisory Committee on Capacitors (1942-1945).

During the Second World War, Sprague invented the Tantalum Capacitor. The use of tantalum allows capacitors to achieve high values of electron storage or capacitance along with higher operating voltages. The big advantage is that the use of tantalum makes the capacitor a fraction of the size of a more conventional design. This aids in cutting space size. Tantalum Capacitors are still used today.
Vishay Intertechnology, which currently owns the Sprague capacitor property rights, calls their tantalum capacitors the *Sprague tantalum*.

Post World War II

After the Second World War, Sprague Electric retooled for the commercial and industrial products market and eventually Sprague capacitors and resistive products became a trusted brand name. Radio and television manufacturers like RCA, Zenith and Philco continued to use Sprague Electric products. Sprague Electric products were also found in stores selling electronic parts, and the electronics servicing business. In 1946 Howard W. Sams (SAMS Publishing) introduced their Photofact Servicing manuals, which were a valuable resource for the service of consumer electronics. Sprague Electric capacitors were listed as a recommended replacement part.

Sprague Electric flourished during the Cold War and the Space Race because of their reputation and experience in the building of military components. By 1954 most of Sprague Electric's sales and profits were from the TV and radio markets, military products sales were second. Sales reached almost $50 million. Also in 1954, the company built new capacitor plants in North Carolina and in the US Territory of Puerto Rico. It was the beginning of Robert C. Sprague's dream to make Sprague Electric into a major corporation; this expansion would continue into the late 1960s.

Sales of Sprague Electric products remained steady from 1954-1958 at just below $50 million. The company continued to expand its product base by opening a semiconductor plant in New Hampshire in 1957 and a magnetics plant in California. As the company grew, union membership (Independent Condenser Workers Union #2) grew as well. By November 1956 straight hourly workers wages were tied to the Bureau of Labor Statistics Consumer Price Index. Additionally, workers received better benefits. The *Sprague Log* recorded in this in a "Special Negotiations Supplement."

Sprague Electric: Expansion, Growth and Difficulties (1960-1971)

By 1959 Sprague Electric achieved $50 million in sales. Robert C. Sprague continued as Chairman of the Board and his brother Julian as President. Contemporary advances in the integrated circuit and thin film technologies, Sprague saw a need to move to support and design products around these new technologies. Thin film products and integrated circuits lead to more compact circuit designs and smaller products. Sprague understood this as the future trend in electronics; he opened more plants in the United States and developed a world wide network of sales offices.

By 1960 Sprague Electric had manufacturing plants in North Carolina, New Hampshire, Vermont, Wisconsin, Virginia, Maryland and California. Many were involved in making capacitors that used thin film technology. This proved to be a very important product for Sprague Electric. These plants also produced magnetic products (transformers, inductors etc.). With advances in transistor and integrated circuit technology (later computer chips) resistance to noise interference became a factor. Magnetics played a role in reducing noise interference.

Sprague got into the semiconductor business in the late 1950s, somewhat later than the already established semiconductor firms. Fairchild Camera (directed by Robert Noyce) had marketed the first commercial integrated circuit as early as 1963. Sprague wanted to be an early participant into this young product. They set up a group at the New Hampshire facility where thin film capacitors were made. In 1965 Sprague Electric acquired Micro Tech (Sunnyvale, CA), a manufacturer of semiconductor equipment for fabrication.
By 1966 Sprague opened a brand new facility in Worcester, MA dedicated to semiconductor and integrated circuit fabrication. The new factory was headed by Dr. John L. Sprague, the youngest son of Robert C. Sprague. John Sprague was a graduate of Stanford University, and specialized in semiconductor development.

Eventually the Micro Tech was moved to the same area. However Sprague's plans for Micro Tech never blossomed, and they wound up making capacitors.[2] Robert C. Sprague's heavy investment in the semiconductor business reduced income for the company.

Sales of Sprague Electric products were $100 million by 1966 and the workforce increased to over 12,000.[4] As the company grew, management was reorganized, and more expansion occurred, in the form of external partnerships.[5] However, this rapid expansion served to keep profits down. Additionally, expansion did not have much impact on wages, benefits and working conditions. As one local historian put it, Robert Sprague's view of his employees was "paternalistic". In March 1970 a major labor strike started and affected all areas of the company. The strike lasted 10 weeks and was ultimately settled by a federal mediator. While Robert C. Sprague and the Union representatives shook hands after the settlement, the results had a negative effect on future of the company, its management and employees.

Sprague Electric: Later years (1970-1978)

With the end of the 1970 strike, Robert C. Sprague retired as chief executive and was succeeded by Neal W. Welch. Although the workers got some of what they demanded, the strike and the new contract would devastate the company. Sprague Electric made cuts to minimize costs, including reducing the labor force and shuttering some of its North Adams operations. Employee morale plummeted which was reflected in the rapid decline of the company's newsletter the *Sprague Log* during this period.[6] The paper was only published twice a year, then not all until 1978. In 1978, the company was sold to General Cable, which later was taken over by Penn Central in 1981.

Closing of the North Adams facility and its future

In the 1980s, Sprague Electric was a division of Penn Central. In 1981, John L. Sprague, the younger son of Robert C. Sprague, was named chief executive.[1] John Sprague tried to bring the employees and management closer together. The *Sprague Log* increased its frequency of publication, and again emphasized the need to work together. During his leadership, sales of Sprague Electric products still grew steadily but not the company's profits. Capacitor products from overseas as well as other electrical and electronic components were cutting into sales from US manufacturers.[7] Also by the 1980s, many electronic assembly plants were overseas, and there was more inclination to buy local or from areas closer to assembly. This was an area Sprague Electric could not compete. Even though sales of Sprague products reached $500 million in the mid-1980s, the Sprague division continue to reorganize. In 1985, it was announced that the Sprague division headquarters would move to Lexington, Massachusetts, and the North Adams, MA plant would close down. As a company Penn Central focused on profits, and Sprague Electric wasn't profitable. As a result, Sprague Electric operations were gradually closed or sold off. Many of the capacitor products were sold in 1993 to Vishay, a leading manufacturer of components used in electronics for industrial and military/space applications.

After Sprague Electric's permanent closing in North Adams, the population of North Adams dropped by 4,000 and the unemployment climbed to 14%. The biggest employer was gone and the site was rusting and decaying. Removal and cleanup of the industrial waste were also issues.

Robert C. Sprague died at home in Williamstown, Mass on September 27, 1991.

Mystique of Sprague Capacitors

With the revival of interest in vacuum tube amplifiers comes the mystique of having the right components for top performance. Sprague Electric components had a long history of name recognition, quality and brand loyalty.

In the early 1950s Sprague produced the "Black Beauty" line of capacitors. These paper capacitors were similar to Robert Sprague's original patent. Instead of using wax coating on the outer body to keep moisture out (moisture renders capacitors useless), Sprague used a resin material to encapsulate the device and provide better and longer lasting resistance to moisture.

In the late 1960s capacitors developed quickly as better materials, such as mylar, were used in their production. Capacitors became more reliable, smaller and able to stand higher voltages Sprague Electric's "Orange Drop" capacitors were well received by manufacturers and designers. They set the standard for "modern" capacitors in appearance and performance. Television circuit boards with Orange Drop capacitors can still be found. Today some designers and restorers will only use Sprague/ Vishay Orange Drops or any Sprague Capacitor.[4] After the breakup of Sprague Electric, the Orange Drop Capacitor line was continued by SBE Inc until 2012, when the Orange Drop product line was sold by SBE to Cornell Dubilier.

Vishay Sprague

Vishay Sprague is well known for having invented the first tantalum capacitors and the first surface-mount tantalum chip capacitors. Vishay Sprague continues this commitment to innovation today through the ongoing development of higher performance tantalum capacitors in a wide range of sizes.

With its MicroTan® family, which is built on a unique assembly process, Vishay Sprague offers the smallest tantalum capacitors on the market with the highest capacitance and voltage ratings. The high-energy HE3 wet tantalum capacitor covers the high side of the capacitance spectrum for wet tantalum capacitors, while other types of wet tantalum capacitors can be found in such extreme applications as military, avionics, space, and oil-drilling.

Vishay Sprague has the broadest range of tantalum capacitors offered by any manufacturer with devices that also include conformal coated and molded surface-mount styles, as well as both radial and axial through-hole products, covering a wide range of automotive, consumer, industrial, and telecommunications as well as very high-performance applications.
Vishay acquired its tantalum capacitor division from Sprague in 1992, which was founded in 1926 by Robert Sprague, founder of the "tone control" capacitor.

Vishay subsequently reinforced its position in the marketplace by acquiring tantalum operations from brands like Mepco, Roederstein, Tansitor, North American Capacitor Company (Mallory capacitors) and more recently, Kemet and Arcotronics wet tantalum products. Vishay is the number one manufacturer of wet tantalum and conformal-coated capacitors worldwide.

Roderick Sprague

Born	Roderick Sprague III February 18, 1933 Albany, Oregon, U.S.
Died	August 20, 2012 (aged 79) Moscow, Idaho
Other names	*Rick*
Residence	Moscow, Idaho
Nationality	United States
Fields	Anthropology, archeology, and ethnohistory
Institutions	University of Arizona (1960–64) Washington State University (1965–67) University of Idaho (1967–97)
Alma mater	Washington State University (B.A.; 1955, M.A.; 1959) University of Arizona (Ph.D., 1967)
Known for	Important contributions to anthropology and archeology
Spouse	Linda Sprague
Children	3 sons, 1 daughter

Roderick Sprague III (February 18, 1933 - August 20, 2012) was a renowned American anthropologist, ethnohistorian and historical archaeologist, and the Emeritus Director of the Laboratory of Anthropology at the University of Idaho in Moscow, where he taught for thirty years. He had extensive experience in environmental impact research, trade beads, aboriginal burial customs, and the Columbia Basin area.

In addition to his work in the traditional anthropological fields, he also collaborated with Professor Grover Krantz in an attempt to apply scientific reasoning to the study of Sasquatch.

Education

Sprague received both his bachelor's and master's degrees in anthropology from Washington State University in Pullman, serving in the U.S. Army in between. He received his Ph.D in 1967 from the University of Arizona in Tucson.

As a graduate student in 1964 at Washington State University, he was the field supervisor of a dig at the Palus burial site in Lyons Ferry, Washington when one of only a few known Jefferson Peace Medals was discovered.

Additionally, his dissertation, "Aboriginal burial practices in the plateau region of North America" (1967) is considered one of the best writings on the topic.

Career

Sprague's career was varied and took him in different directions. He conducted excavations in the Pacific Northwest, Alaska, and the Canadian Maritime on Prince Edward Island; and research in the American Southwest and Inner Mongolia. Much of his research was on burial practices and historical archaeology, with a special interest in glass and ceramic trade beads and buttons. He conducted burial research at the request of ten different American Indian tribal governments. Sprague was an early advocate of the importance of repatriation in archaeological and anthropological excavations, long before the enactment of the Native American Graves Protection and Repatriation Act.

Sprague served many roles in the Society for Historical Archaeology: on the Board of Directors from 1970–71, secretary-treasurer from 1971–1974, member of the Editorial Advisory Board since 1977, Book Review Editor from 1977 to 1997, Archivist from 1987 to 1998, as President in 1976 and 1990 and as Parliamentarian from 1984 to 2008.

He was a Professor of Anthropology at the University of Idaho in Moscow for thirty years, until his retirement in 1997.

Sprague, along with Dr. Deward E. Walker, founded the scholarly journal Northwest Anthropological Research Notes in 1966, called the Journal of Northwest Anthropology since 2001.

Awards

Sprague was the first member of The Society for Historical Archaeology to be awarded both the J. C. Harrington Medal in Historical Archaeology and the Carol Ruppe Distinguished Service Award.

Personal life

In retirement, Sprague lived in Moscow with his wife Linda, who also holds degrees in anthropology. He had four adult children: Roderick IV, Katherine, Frederick, and Alexander Sprague.

Published works

- Burial Terminology: A Guide For Researchers (Lanham: AltaMira Press, 2005, ISBN 0-7591-0841-2)
- Excavations at the Warren Chinese mining camp site, with Michael Striker, Moscow: Alfred W. Bowers Laboratory of Anthropology, University of Idaho, 1993.
- A Preliminary Bibliography of Washington Archaeology Pullman: Washington State University, 1967)
- The Material Culture of Steamboat Passengers - Archaeological Evidence from the Missouri River (New York: Springer, 1999, Annalies Corbin 0306461684)
- A Bibliography of Trade Beads in North America, with Karlis Karklins. Promontory Press, 1987. 0969276109
- The Descriptive Archaeology of the Palus Burial Site, Lyons Ferry, Washington, Pullman: Washington State University, 1965. B0007HGKL4

Among his published works on Sasquatch:

- The Scientist Looks at the Sasquatch (Moscow: University Press of Idaho, 1977, with anthropologist Grover Krantz)
- The Scientist Looks at the Sasquatch II (Moscow: University Press of Idaho, 1979, also with Grover Krantz, ISBN 0-89301-061-8)

R. B. Sprague

Born	September 12, 1937 Buffalo, New York
Died	28 July 2010 (aged 72) Santa Fe, NM
Education	El Dorado High School, University of Oklahoma
Known for	Painter, Drawings
Movement	Realist
Awards	1992 C. Howard Wilkins, Sr. Award, Witchita Art Association 1962 Elmer Capshaw Award for Excellence in Graphics, He was honored as Artist in Residence at the University of Oklahoma in 2001

R. B. (Roger) Sprague (September 12, 1937 - July 28, 2010) was an American Contemporary Realist artist.

Sprague was born in Buffalo, New York, and raised in south Arkansas, graduating from El Dorado High School. He attended the University of Oklahoma and graduated with a BA in Fine Arts, with majors in botany, architecture, and finally, in painting. Sprague resided in New York City and worked as booking agent and shipboard companion for United States Lines. He lived for a year on Swan's Island,

Maine, where his father's family started life in the U.S. His conviction to make art his life and his living came to fruition in 1975 when he moved to New Mexico, working briefly in Bosque Farms in a plant nursery, then moving to a one room arrangement in Santa Fe in 1979 where he dedicated his life to his art.

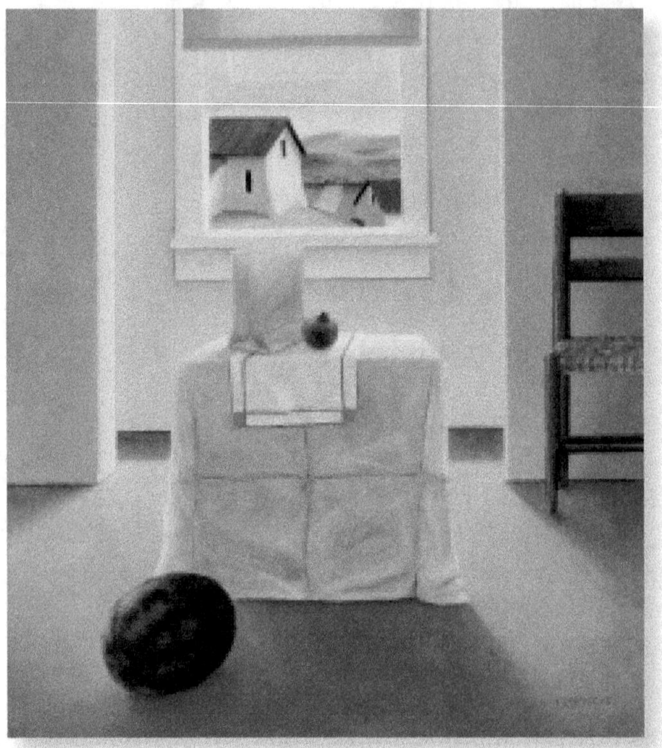

In 2010, Patricia Rovzar Gallery said:
R.B. Sprague is driven by his never-ending exploration of scale and light. Painting in oil on linen the majority of Sprague's work focuses on interior spaces and the relationships of the objects he places within those spaces. He defines his compositions with common objects like tables and chairs but always leaves ample room for the viewer to create their own interpretation.

R.B. Sprague said in Southwest Art: I paint what I see, and what attracts me is light and the geometry it illuminates. When I see light on a surface at a particular moment. I think it will follow me for the rest of my life.

Royal Sprague

Royal Tyler Sprague (born in New Haven, Vermont, Jan. 23, 1814; died Sacramento, California Feb. 24, 1872) was the 11th Chief Justice of California.

Sprague taught elementary school in Potsdam, New York and later opened a school in Zanesville, Ohio. In 1838 he began to study law and was admitted to the bar in Ohio. The finding of gold in the Sierra Nevada prompted Sprague to became a "Forty-Niner". After arriving in California in September 1849, Sprague worked a claim on Clear Creek on the Sacramento River. He settled in Reading's Springs, now Shasta, California, and once again became an attorney. He was elected to the California State Senate in 1852.

Sprague returned to Ohio briefly in 1852 to retrieve his family. He had four children: Anna Maria Sprague (1845–1879); Arthur Hale Sprague (1848–1922); Ella Sprague (1853-5); and Frances Royal Sprague (1864–1957).

Sprague was elected to the Supreme Court of California in 1867 (as a Democrat); he was chosen to be Chief Justice in 1872 and died the same year. He is interred in Sacramento Historic City Cemetery.

A collection of his journals is in the collection of the Bancroft Library at the University of California, Berkeley.

Thomas Bond Sprague

Thomas Bond Sprague (born March 29, 1830, died November 29, 1920) was a British actuary who was the only person to have been President of both the Institute of Actuaries (1882–1886) in London and the Faculty of Actuaries (1894–1896) in Edinburgh, prior to their merger in 2010.

Sprague was an undergraduate at St John's College, Cambridge where he was elected to a fellowship following his ranking as Senior Wrangler in the Cambridge Mathematical Tripos of 1853. He was awarded the Smith's Prize of Cambridge University in the same year. After serving as the actuary to the Equity and Law life insurance company (1861–1873), he became Chief Executive (1873–1900) of the Scottish Equitable Life Assurance Society in Edinburgh. He retired at age 70.

The Thomas Bond Sprague Prize was established in his honour in 2012 within Churchill College, Cambridge and the Faculty of Mathematics, University of Cambridge.

Thomas L. Sprague

Thomas Lamison Sprague	
Born	October 2, 1894 Lima, Ohio
Died	September 17, 1972 (aged 77) Chula Vista, California
Allegiance	United States
Service/branch	United States Navy
Years of service	1917–1952
Rank	Vice Admiral
Commands held	USS *Montgomery* (DD-121) Scouting Squadron 6 USS *Charger* (AVG-30) USS *Intrepid* (CV-11) Carrier Division 22 Task Group 77.4 / Task Unit 77.4.1 ("Taffy I") Carrier Division 11 Carrier Division 3 Task Force 38.1 Pacific Fleet Air Force
Battles/wars	World War I World War II
Awards	Navy Cross Navy Distinguished Service Medal Legion of Merit with Combat "V" and gold star

Thomas Lamison Sprague (October 2, 1894 – September 17, 1972) was a vice admiral of the United States Navy, who served during World War II as commander of the aircraft carrier *Intrepid* (CV-11) and took part in the battles of Guam, Leyte Gulf and Okinawa.

Naval Academy and World War I

Born in Lima, Ohio, Sprague graduated from the United States Naval Academy in 1917 (although no relation to Admiral Clifton "Ziggy" Sprague, the two both attended the Naval Academy, later graduating from the same class). He served aboard the protected cruiser *Cleveland* (C-19) assigned to the trans-Atlantic convoy from June 1917 until April 1918 and, after serving on shore duty for a brief period, Sprague assisted in the official commission of the destroyer *Montgomery* (DD-121) in July. As a member of the ship's anti-submarine patrol, Sprague would eventually come to command the *Montgomery* from January to November 1920.

Inter-war years

After participating in naval flight training at Naval Air Station Pensacola, Sprague served as a staff officer under Pacific Air commander Admiral H.V. Butler from 1921 to 1923. In 1926,

Sprague was transferred to the battleship *Maryland* (BB-46) serving with Observation Squadron 1 for two years before being stationed at the Naval Air Station San Diego in 1928. Between 1931 and 1936, Sprague served as commander of Scouting Squadron 6, director of the Aeronautical Engine Laboratory at the Naval Aircraft Factory in Philadelphia, and air officer on board the carrier *Saratoga* (CV-3) before being reassigned as to Pensacola as superintendent of Naval Air Training from 1937 to 1940.

World War II

Serving as executive officer on board the *Ranger* (CV-4) on the Neutrality Patrol in the Atlantic for a year, Sprague helped commission the escort carrier *Charger* (AVG-30) and commanded the vessel during training missions in the Chesapeake from February to December 1942.

After serving staff duty from January to June 1943, Sprague commissioned the *Intrepid* (CV-11) in August, and commanded the aircraft carrier in raids against the Truk and Marshall Islands during the first two months of 1944.

Promoted to Rear Admiral in June, Sprague commanded Carrier Division 22 which covered the assault on Guam from July–August and Morotai in September. In command of Task Group 77.4 and Task Unit 77.4.1 ("Taffy 1") during the Battle of Leyte Gulf from October 24–25, Sprague briefly commanded Pacific training carriers under Carrier Division 11, before leading Carrier Division 3 off Okinawa from April–June 1945. He commanded Task Force 38.1 during the final air operations against Japan by the war's end.

Post-war career and death

Sprague was named deputy chief, then chief, of the Bureau of Naval Personnel in 1946 serving until his promotion to Vice Admiral in August 1949. Appointed commander of the Pacific Fleet Air Force in October, Sprague would hold this post until his retirement in April 1952. He briefly returned to active duty to negotiate with the Philippine government over the status of U.S. air bases in 1956.

Sprague died at Chula Vista, California on September 17, 1972.

William Sprague

William Sprague (October 26, 1609 - October 26, 1675) left England on the ship Lyon's Whelp for Plymouth/Salem Massachusetts. He was originally from Upwey, near Weymouth, Dorset, England.

William arrived at Naumkeag (Salem) with his brothers Ralph and Richard. They were employed by Governor Endecott to explore and take possession of the country westward. They explored the land over to (present day) Charlestown, Massachusetts, between Mystic and Charles rivers, where they made peace with the local Indians. On February 10, 1634, the order creating a Board of Selectmen was passed, and Richard and William Sprague signed it.

William lived in Charlestown until 1636, before moving to Hingham, where he was one of the first planters. His house lot, on Union St. "over the river" was said to be the pleasantest lot in Hingham. He was active in public affairs, and was constable, fence-viewer, etc.

William's will names his wife, Millicent (Eames), and children, Anthony, Samuel, William, Joan, Jonathan, Persis, Johanna, and Mary.

Other Sprague relatives became soldiers in the American Revolutionary War and two of them, William Sprague III and William Sprague IV, became governors of the state of Rhode Island.

Lucille Ball and her brother, Fred Ball, were direct descendants.

William Sprague III

William Sprague	
United States Senator from Rhode Island	
In office	
February 18, 1842 – January 17, 1844	
14th Governor of Rhode Island	
In office	
May 2, 1838 – May 2, 1839	
Lieutenant	Joseph Childs
Member of the U.S. House of Representatives from Rhode Island's At-large district	
In office	
March 4, 1835 – March 4, 1837	

Personal details	
Born	November 3, 1799 Cranston, Rhode Island
Died	October 19, 1856 (aged 56) Providence, Rhode Island
Political party	Whig

William Sprague, also known as **William III** or **William Sprague III** (November 3, 1799 - October 19, 1856), was a politician and industrialist from the U.S. state of Rhode Island, serving as the 14th Governor, a U.S. Representative and a U.S. Senator. He was the uncle of William Sprague IV, also a Governor and Senator from Rhode Island.

William Sprague was the son of William Sprague 773-1836 and Anna Potter 763-1828. He was born in the Gov. William Sprague Mansion in Cranston, Rhode Island, and pursued classical studies as a student. He engaged in mercantile pursuits and was a member of the Rhode Island House of Representatives, serving as speaker from 1832 to 1835 and leading a coalition of Anti-Masonic and Democratic Party members.

He was elected as an at-large candidate from the Whig Party to the Twenty-fourth Congress and served from March 4, 1835, to March 4, 1837. He declined to be a candidate for renomination in 1836. He was elected Governor of Rhode Island in 1838. He subsequently was elected as a Whig to the United States Senate to fill the vacancy caused by the death of Nathan F. Dixon and served from February 18, 1842, to January 17, 1844, when he resigned. He served as chairman of the U.S. Senate Committee on Enrolled Bills in the Twenty-seventh Congress. He was a U.S. presidential elector on the Whig ticket in 1848.

His family fortune came from the cotton and paint

manufacturing, and he assumed active control of the family business following the murder of his brother Amasa on December 31, 1843. The Senator took an active interest in the trial of the Gordon brothers for the murder. The trial resulted in one of the defendants being sent to the gallows, and remains highly controversial for the amount of anti-Irish bigotry involved. In 2011, the condemned man was posthumously pardoned by the Rhode Island governor.

In addition to the family business, he was president of the Hartford, Providence, and Fishkill Railroad, and of two banks. The extended Sprague family has descendants who live in the Utica, New York area. Sprague died in Providence, Rhode Island, and is interred in Swan Point Cemetery there.

William Sprague (Michigan)

	William Sprague
Born	February 23, 1809 Providence, Rhode Island
Died	September 19, 1868 (aged 59) Kalamazoo, Michigan

William Sprague (February 23, 1809 - September 19, 1868) was a minister and politician in the U.S. state of Michigan. Sprague was born in Providence, Rhode Island, a distant cousin of William Sprague, Governor of Rhode Island. He attended the public schools there, moved to Michigan, and settled in Kalamazoo, where he studied theology and was ordained as a minister. He was presiding elder of the Methodist Episcopal Church, Kalamazoo district, 1844–1848. Sprague served as United States Indian Agent in Michigan 1852–1853.

In the early 1830s, Sprague was a circuit minister for many communities in central and southwest Michigan. He delivered the first gospel sermon ever given in Van Buren County, Michigan, in the first log cabin which was built in spring 1829. He organized the first Methodist class in Niles in 1832 and was pastor there in 1862 when construction began on a historical Italianate style church building. In the fall of 1832, Sprague became circuit pastor for Coldwater.

Sprague defeated incumbent Democrat Charles E. Stuart to be elected as a Whig, though he is sometimes also identified with the Free Soil Party, from Michigan's 2nd District to the Thirty-first Congress, serving March 4, 1849–March 3, 1851. He did not run for re-election. He retired to his farm in Oshtemo Township, Kalamazoo County. He died in Kalamazoo.

William P. Sprague

William Peter Sprague
Member of the U.S. House of Representatives from Ohio's 15th district
In office
March 4, 1871 – March 3, 1875
Member of the Ohio Senate from the 14th district
In office
January 2, 1860 – January 3, 1864
Personal details

Born	May 21, 1827 Malta, Ohio
Died	March 3, 1899 (aged 71) McConnelsville, Ohio
Resting place	Riverview Cemetery, McConnelsville
Political party	Republican

William Peter Sprague (May 21, 1827 - March 3, 1899) was a businessman, banker, politician, and a two-term U.S. Representative from Ohio.

Sprague was born near Malta in Morgan County, Ohio, and attended the country schools. He engaged in mercantile pursuits when quite young and continued in active business until 1864.

He was a member of the Ohio Senate from 1860 to 1863 during the American Civil War. He moved to McConnelsville, Ohio, in 1866 and engaged in banking. He was elected as a Republican to the Forty-second and Forty-third Congresses (March 4, 1871 - March 3, 1875). Sprague was not a candidate for renomination in 1874 and subsequently resumed the banking business in Malta.

He died in McConnelsville and was buried in Riverview Cemetery.

William Sprague IV

William Sprague	
United States Senator from Rhode Island	
In office	
March 4, 1863 – March 3, 1875	
In office	
May 29, 1860 – March 3, 1863	
Lieutenant	J. Russell Bullock Samuel G. Arnold Seth Padelford
Personal details	
Born	September 12, 1830 Cranston, Rhode Island, U.S.

Died	September 11, 1915 (aged 84) Paris, France
Resting place	Swan Point Cemetery
Political party	Republican
Spouse(s)	Kate Chase Dora Inez Clavert
Profession	Politician, Manufacturer

William Sprague IV (September 12, 1830 - September 11, 1915) was the 27th Governor of Rhode Island from 1860 to 1863, and U.S. Senator from 1863 to 1875. He participated in the First Battle of Bull Run during the American Civil War.

Early years

Sprague was born in the Gov. William Sprague Mansion in Cranston, Rhode Island, the youngest son of Amasa and Fanny Morgan Sprague. His uncle and namesake William Sprague III was also a Governor and U.S. Senator as well as U.S. Representative from Rhode Island. William and brother Amasa's education at the Irving Institute in Tarrytown, New York, was cut short when their father was murdered on New Year's Eve in 1843 in Knightsville, Rhode Island. The murder was considered a major event of the period, and the trial of accused killer John Gordon was marked by anti-Irish bigotry; Gordon was subsequently found guilty and executed.

Both brothers were called to work in the family business, the A.& W. Sprague Manufacturing Company, which was then under the direction of their uncle William III. When their uncle died in 1856, William and Amasa - along with their cousin Col. Byron Sprague, son of William III, and their mother Fanny Sprague and Aunt Harriet, widow of William

III - became partners in the company. The second incorporation of the A. & W. Sprague Company occurred on June 2, 1859. It soon was the largest calico printing textile mill in the world. The company ran five weaving mills in New England. The Hartford, Providence and Fishkill Railroad - of which William III had purchased controlling interest - connected the five mills to the Sprague Print Works in Cranston. The woven cloth was brought to Cranston to be printed. Sprague later became interested in linen weaving and locomotive building.

Politics

Like his uncle, William Sprague IV had an interest in politics and was elected in 1860 as the Rhode Island Union Party candidate for Governor over the Republican Party whose candidate was seen as too radical. He was re-elected in 1861 and 1862. At twenty-nine years old, he was the youngest governor of a state at that time. He was sometimes referred to as the "boy governor," a title he may have given himself while campaigning for election.

As the Civil War approached, Sprague promised U.S. President Abraham Lincoln the support of Rhode Island. Upon Lincoln's call for volunteers in April 1861, a brigade of two infantry regiments was raised by Rhode Island. Sprague, believing that the war would last only 48 hours, accompanied the Rhode Island brigade, under command of Colonel Ambrose Burnside, in the First Battle of Bull Run on July 21, 1861. During the battle, Sprague acted as and aide to General Burnside and had his horse shot from under him. The Confederate victory made it clear to Sprague that the war would last longer than two days. Although he was offered a commission as a Brigadier General of Volunteers on August 9, 1861, he declined the appointment to focus on his duties as governor.

In 1862, he attended the Loyal War Governors' Conference in Altoona, Pennsylvania, which ultimately backed Abraham Lincoln's Emancipation Proclamation and the Union war effort. Retiring from the governor's office in 1863, he was elected by the state Senate to two six year terms as US Senator from Rhode Island, taking office on March 4, 1863 and serving until March 3, 1875. He served as chairman of the committees on public lands and on manufactures and as a member of the committees on commerce and on military affairs.

Innovations and Ideas

After leaving the Senate, he resumed the direction of his manufacturing establishments. He operated the first rotary machine for making horseshoes, perfected a mowing machine, and also various processes in calico printing, especially that of direct printing on a large scale with the extract of madder without a chemical bath. Sprague claimed to have discovered what he called the "principle of the orbit as inherent in social forces." He asserted that money is endowed with two tendencies, the distributive and the aggregative. When the aggregative tendency predominates, as before the Civil War, decadence results; but when the distributive tendency is in the ascendancy, as it was later in the 19th century, there is progress.

Marriage to Kate Chase

William and Kate Sprague

On November 12, 1863, Sprague married Kate Chase, daughter of Secretary of the Treasury Salmon P. Chase. She was considered the belle of Washington. Sprague's wedding gift to Kate was a tiara of matched pearls and diamonds that cost more than $50,000. As the bride entered the room, the Marine Band played "The Kate Chase March" which composer

Thomas Mark Clark had written for the occasion. Although their marriage began well, quarreling became more common. They had four children: William (b. 1865), Ethel (b. 1869), Catherine ("Kitty," b. 1871) (who was mentally disabled) and Portia (b. 1873).

William's financial and political fortunes rapidly deteriorated in 1873, with the financial panic. His holdings were extensive both in Rhode Island and nationally. The death of his father-in-law, Salmon P. Chase, in the same year who had become Chief Justice of the United States, added to his family problems. Severe setbacks occurred to the A. & W. Sprague Company following the Panic of 1873. Likewise, the Spragues' marriage unravelled as William began to drink more, had affairs with other women and began to criticize Kate's spending. Kate allegedly had an affair with New York senator Roscoe Conkling. According to popular rumor, in 1879 Sprague chased Conkling off his Narragansett estate after catching him with Kate, thus ending the alleged affair.

The couple divorced in 1882. William stayed with his father and the daughters lived with Kate Chase, who took back her maiden name after the divorce. After spending some time in Europe, Kate lived with her daughters outside Washington, D.C. at Edgewood, her father's estate. When her only son Willie Sprague took his own life at age 25 in 1890, Kate Chase became a recluse. She died in poverty in 1899.

Marriage to Dora Inez Clavert

Following his divorce, William Sprague married Dora Inez Clavert of West Virginia in Staunton, Virginia, in 1883. He regained his interest in politics to become the first Narragansett, Rhode Island Town Council President in 1900. On October 11, 1909, a fire destroyed the Sprague mansion, including Sprague's diaries and other valuable artifacts. The Spragues moved to Paris. During World War I, they opened their apartment as a convalescent hospital for the wounded of all nationalities.

Sprague died of complications from meningitis on September 11, 1915, a day short of his 85th birthday. Following simple funeral services in France, his wife arranged for his body to be brought back to Rhode Island draped in an American flag. He received full military honors when laid to rest in the family tomb at Swan Point Cemetery in Providence, Rhode Island. He was the last living senator who had served during the Civil War.

Lucille Ball

[Editor: While not a Sprague by name, Lucy is probably the most well known celebrity that can trace her ancestry directly to the Sprague line (in Upwey, Dorset, England). Lucy was aware of, and proud of her heritage of being descended from the Spragues that helped found America.]

Born	Lucille Désirée Ball August 6, 1911 Jamestown, New York, U.S.
Died	April 26, 1989 (aged 77) Beverly Hills, California
Cause of death	Abdominal aortic dissection
Other names	Lucille Ball Morton Lucille Ball Arnaz Diane Belmont Lucy Ball Lucy Arnaz Lucy Morton
Occupation	Actress, comedian, model, film executive
Years active	1932–1989
Spouse(s)	Desi Arnaz (m. 1940; div. 1960) Gary Morton (m. 1961; her death 1989)
Children	Lucie Arnaz Desi Arnaz Jr.
Signature	

Lucille Désirée Ball (August 6, 1911 – April 26, 1989) was an American actress, comedian, model, and film studio executive. She was the star of the sitcoms *I Love Lucy*, *The Lucy–Desi*

Comedy Hour, *The Lucy Show*, *Here's Lucy*, and *Life with Lucy*.

Ball's career in the spotlight began in 1929, when she landed work as a model. Shortly thereafter, Lucille began her performing career on Broadway using the stage name Diane Belmont and Dianne Belmont. She performed many small movie roles in the 1930s and 1940s as a contract player for RKO Radio Pictures, being cast as a chorus girl, or in similar roles, and was dubbed the "Queen of the Bs" (referring to her many roles in B-films). In the midst of her work as a control player for RKO, Ball met Cuban bandleader Desi Arnaz. The two eloped in 1940.

During the 1950s, Lucille Ball became a television star. In 1951, Ball and Arnaz created the television series *I Love Lucy*, a show that would go on to be one of the most beloved programs in television history. On July 17, 1951, at almost forty years of age, Ball gave birth to their first child, Lucie Désirée Arnaz. A year and a half later, she gave birth to their second child, Desiderio Alberto Arnaz IV, known as Desi Arnaz, Jr. Ball and Arnaz divorced on May 4, 1960.

In 1962, Ball became the first woman to run a major television studio, Desilu. Her studio produced many successful and popular television series, including *Mission: Impossible* and *Star Trek*. She continued making film and television appearances for most of the rest of her life, albeit without ever attaining the success she enjoyed in the 1950s.
Ball was nominated for an Emmy Award thirteen times and won four times. In 1977, Ball was among the first recipients of the Women in Film Crystal Award. She was the recipient of the Golden Globe Cecil B. DeMille Award in 1979, the Lifetime Achievement Award from the Kennedy Center Honors in 1986, and the Governors Award from the Academy of Television Arts & Sciences in 1989.

On April 26, 1989, Ball died of an abdominal aortic dissection at the age of seventy-seven.[0] At the time of her death, she had been married to standup comedian Gary Morton, her business partner and second husband, for more than twenty-seven years.

William Sprague (1609–1675)

William Sprague (October 26, 1609 - October 26, 1675) left England on the ship Lyon's Whelp for Plymouth/Salem Massachusetts. He was originally from Upwey, near Weymouth, Dorset, England.

William arrived at Naumkeag (Salem) with his brothers Ralph and Richard. They were employed by Governor Endecott to explore and take possession of the country westward. They explored the land over to (present day) Charlestown, Massachusetts, between Mystic and Charles rivers, where they made peace with the local Indians. On February 10, 1634, the order creating a Board of Selectmen was passed, and Richard and William Sprague signed it.

William lived in Charlestown until 1636, before moving to Hingham, where he was one of the first planters. His house lot, on Union St. "over the river" was said to be the pleasantest lot in Hingham. He was active in public affairs, and was constable, fence-viewer, etc. William's will names his wife, Millicent (Eames), and children, Anthony, Samuel, William, Joan, Jonathan, Persis, Johanna, and Mary.

Other Sprague relatives became soldiers in the American Revolutionary War and two of them, William Sprague III and William Sprague IV, became governors of the state of Rhode Island.

Lucille Ball and her brother, Fred Ball, were direct descendants.

Sprague History & Artifacts

Lyon's Whelp

In 1628, the very wealthy Duke of Buckingham built a private fleet of 10 three-masted, armed full rigged pinnaces, each of which carried the name *Lion's Whelp*. At least one *Lion's Whelp* participated in the English attempt to relieve the Huguenot citadel of La Rochelle during the Anglo-French War. Little information has survived about the careers of the other *Lion's Whelps* and they disappear from the historical record in 1654. Important documents about their finance and construction have survived and made a lasting contribution to our understanding of the Navy Royal during the early 17th century.

Lion's Whelp, 1628	
Career (England)	
Name:	*Lion's Whelp*
Ordered:	February 28, 1628
Laid down:	March 1628
Launched:	late July, 1628
Acquired:	Duke of Buckingham, July, 1628; Royal Navy, 1632
Commissioned:	1632
In service:	1628 to 1632 to 1654
Out of service:	1628 to 1632 to 1654
Fate:	Various
Notes:	John Graves built eighth and ninth *Whelps*. Phineas Pett's certificates of works done have survived for all *Whelps* except the ninth.
General characteristics	
Type:	3-masted pinnace, auxiliary oared warship
Displacement:	186 tons 180 long tons (183 t)
Beam:	25 ft (7.6 m)
Depth of hold:	9 ft (2.7 m)

Propulsion:	Sweeps (two oars between each cannon port)
Armament:	9 broadside cannons, 2 sternchase gunports
Notes:	The *Whelps* were classed as ships "of the sixth rank"

Introduction

The 10 *Lion's Whelps* built by the 1st Duke of Buckingham in 1628 are exemplars of the 'war' pinnace, a war ship that was built for several European navies for more than two centuries (c.1550-c.1750). The Whelps had sweeps (propelling oars) as well as sails (G R Balleine, All for the King, The Life Story of Sir George Carteret, Societe Jersiase, 1976, p10). England, the Netherlands, Sweden and Poland deployed the war pinnace on a regular basis. The largest war pinnaces, also known as frigates, approximated England's fifth rate and sixth rate small warships. A few war pinnaces were built to fourth-rate hull dimensions. However, these war pinnaces carried fewer cannon and had smaller crews than English fourth, fifth, and sixth rates. Fast and maneuverable when compared to a typical ship of the line, when they were under the command of an experienced captain with a crew that retained discipline during battle, many war pinnaces compiled impressive fighting and espionage records.

Ten ships of the name *Lyon's Whelp* were built in 1628 by George Villiers, 1st Duke of Buckingham, and each was constructed to the same design. Although masted and armed from the stores of the Royal Navy, the fleet was paid for by the Duke. The entire fleet of ten *Lion's Whelps* cost Buckingham about £7,000 and for several years, they were his private fleet. With the exception of the Earl of Pembroke, the

Duke of Buckingham was the wealthiest nobleman in England at this time. This ship building program indicates that the Duke of Buckingham could access very significant funds. The Duke spent £7000 in 1628 to build his fleet which in the first quarter of 2011 would be worth £624,120.00.

Under the Duke's command, the *Lion's Whelps* were privateers dedicated to increasing his considerable personal fortune. The fleet of ten *Lions Whelps* was not taken over by the Navy until 1632, after Buckingham's assassination in 1628, and compensation of at least £4000 was paid to his estate.

The Earl of Nottingham

Lyon's Whelp was the name given to several British naval ships dating back to the 16th century, including at least two that were not financed or built by the Duke of Buckingham. The immediate predecessor to Buckingham's fleet of 10 *Lion's Whelps* was a war ship named *Lion's Whelp* that was owned by Charles Howard, 1st Earl of Nottingham, who was the Lord High Admiral of England (1585–1619) and who was succeeded by the Duke of Buckingham.

This *Lion's Whelp* was loaned to Sir Walter Raleigh and joined the English fleet for the combined Anglo-Dutch attack and expected capture of Cadiz in 1596.[Note 5 Robert Devereux, 2nd Earl of Essex and Sir Walter Raleigh were among the commanders of landing forces while Sir Charles Howard as admiral led the fleet. Victory was swift because the Spanish fleet had been set afire in order not be captured and their land army was badly organized. The Dutch and English sacked and pillaged Cadiz all the while respecting its citizens much to the astonishment of the Spanish. This *Lion's Whelp* was sold to the state in 1602, and then repaired at Chatham by the ambitious young shipwright Phineas Pett (see below). The Duke of

Buckingham received this *Lion's Whelp* as a gift from King James VI in 1625, shortly before the King died. Ratification of the transfer of ownership occurred under King Charles.

Warrants, contracts, and shipbuilders

Several years ago, John Wassell worked with the Public Record Office in London and England's Calendars of State Papers to research the ten *Lion's Whelps* built by the Duke of Buckingham in 1628. His web page presents the most important information obtained - original period documents from the archive "State Papers, Domestic". Each *Whelp* had one gun deck, two masts with a rig that included square sails and lateen. There are only a few contemporary drawings and paintings of English war pinnaces or frigates of the Jacobean era. Details of hull design, armament and rigging are usually inferred using prints and hull designs of warships in the Dutch Navy.

The Duke of Buckingham's project to build 10 *Lion's Whelps* began with his warrant to two well-placed friends. Captain Sir John Penington and Phineas Pett ensured that the ablest shipwrights of the region would be available for the building of this fleet. Their basic design was a warship of 125 tons with both sails and oars ('sweeps'). Ship construction would be done on the banks of the River Thames, particularly at Ipswich and Shorum. The Lord Admiral was to oversee the "preparation and setting out" for 10 pinnaces of 120 tons each. (Each *Lion's Whelp* was built to 186 tons.. see below.) Each ship was to have a tender, and adequate supplies of oars, cable, anchors, sails, canvas and 'all other tackling and rigging to be furnished from his 'Majesties Stores', likewise for ordnance and ammunition. "Their Lordships well approving of the said motion did think fit and order the same accordingly." The motive for building these ten ships was the 'enterprise of La

Rochelle'. These ten ships would be added to the English fleet that would undertake to relieve the siege of the French Hugenot (Protestant) center of power at La Rochelle as imposed by King Louis XIII. Considerable resources must have been available because Phinaeus Pett left this employment at the end of July, which indicates that the ten ships had been completed and launched by that time (~6 months) or shortly thereafter. Thereupon the Duke's fleet set sail for Portsmouth and assignments with the Royal Navy. The group that met at Whitehall on February 27, 1627 was impressive. The heart of England's political and military power was present: Lord Keeper (of the privy seal)- Lord Treasurer - Lord President (of the council) - Lord Admiral - Lord Steward - Earl of Suffolk - Earl of Dorset - Earl of Exeter - Earl of Morton - Earl of Kelley - Viscount Wimbledon - Viscount Grandison - Mr. Treasurer – Master of the Ward(robe) - Mr. Chanc(ellor) of the Exchequer - Mr Chanc. of the Duchy (of Lancaster).

Although there are no surviving remains of any of the ten *Lion's Whelps* built by the Duke of Buckingham, it is possible to obtain a portrait of these ships. Dutch marine painters of the period often included detailed examples of Dutch, English and Spanish ships in their paintings. A small oil-on-copper painting by Abraham de Verwer c.1625, that is now in the England's National Maritime Museum, shows Dutch and English war pinnaces saluting each other outside a harbour. The English ship is a good fit to the reconstructed profile for a Buckingham *Lion's Whelp* as a three-masted war pinnace with a single gun deck that had eight broadside cannon ports. There is a grating or 'flying deck' over the waist, and Royal Arms decorated the stern. There is another and similar painting of an English single deck war pinnace in the National Maritime Museum.

The Anglo-French War

At least one of Buckingham's ten *Lion's Whelps* saw service with the British Fleet in England's attempt to relieve the Huguenot citadel of La Rochelle. English action in the Anglo-French War began with a siege of the fortress of Saint-Martin-de-Re in 1627. The English fleet was not able to lay siege to La Rochelle until several months later.

Historians are indebted to Jacques Callot who published a series of prints illustrating the English landing on the Isle de Re at the beach of Sablanceau, the Siege of Saint Martin-de-Re and the Siege of La Rochelle.[Note 7 Callot's technical innovations enhanced the detail in his prints. In his portrayal of the English fleet, it is possible to differentiate galleons, carracks, pinnaces and perhaps shallops becauise each ship type had the same minute iconic image. Peraps one of the pinnaces in these prints is Buckingham's sixth *Lion's Whelp.*

The besotted King James I assigned a central role to his favorite courtier with the expedition to relieve the stronghold of La Rochelle (Hugenot). England hoped that a success would bring the French Protestants into an alliance against Catholic Spain and provide a demonstration of English naval power that would leave King Louis XIII hesitant and fearful. English King James I had made George Villiers, Lord Admiral of the Royal Navy in 1619. As an important commander during the Siege of Saint-Martin-de-Ré (1627) and the attempt to relieve La Rochelle, the Duke of Buckingham revealed a serious lack of understanding and expertise when faced with both army and naval strategic challenges.

The siege of Saint-Martin-de-Ré was the first action in this attempt to take La Rochelle and it began when Buckingham's fleet landed troops on the beach at Sablanceau. Apparently Buckingham insisted on an orderly, slow and methodical organization of his army on the exposed beach, even as French troops and cavalry made repeated lightning attacks, emerging from the protection of the sand dunes. About 100 English casualties on the beach were unnecessary. Later, it was revealed that Buckingham's preparations for the siege of Saint Martin included ladders that proved too short to reach the top of Saint-Martin-de-Re's walls.

After three months, Buckingham called off the Siege of Saint-Martin. He retreatedto Loix, then sailed home to England, defeated and humiliated.

English strategy correctly viewed the fortress of Saint-Martin-de-Re as a serious impediment to an assault on La Rochelle. With 80 ships and 7,000 men, Buckingham failed to take the fortress city. After three months and a final failed assault on October 27, 1627, he ended the siege and left for England from Loix with a demoralized, disease ridden force of 2,000 men, the survivors of his original army of 7,000 men.

A *Lion's Whelp* to Massachusetts

In 1629 a *Lion's Whelp* sailed with four other ships from Gravesend on April 25, 1629 for the Massachusetts Bay Colony. Arrived and greeted by Governor John Endecott on June 30, 1629. All ships were armed merchantmen. Eight cannon were listed for this *Lion's Whelp* which is the number carried by the Duke of Buckingham's *Lion's Whelps* and most armed pinnaces as well. Is this ship Buckingham's second *Lion's Whelp*, diverted for a cross Atlantic run with settlers and provisions to the Massachusetts Bay Colony? A careful scrutiny of the record is not supportive of this conclusion. This *Lion's Whelp* is tentatively identified as the 120-ton ship that brought William Dodge, along with the Sprague family and others to Salem, Massachusetts in 1629. The *Lyon's Whelp* left Gravesend 24/25 April 1629 and arrived in Salem mid-July 1629, under Master John Gibbs (or Gibbon). It was one of six ships in a small fleet; the others including the Talbot, *George Bonaventure*, *Lyon*, and a ship called the *Mayflower* (though not the *Mayflower* of the Pilgrims). This *Lion's Whelp* and her sister ships the *Talbot* and the *George* carried goods and new settlers to Naumkaeg, the Indian name for the territory settled by England's Massachusetts Bay Company at Salem.

10 Lion's Whelps

Final costings for each *Lion's Whelp* are believed to have been in excess of the contracted rate, thereby raising the possibility that shipwrights deliberately built ships larger than agreed upon in order to inflate the final invoice. The worse example of this was Peter Pett and the sixth *Whelp*. The Duke wanted each *Whelp* to weigh 120 tonnes, and cost £139.5.

After the Duke was assassinated in 1632, his fleet of ten *Lion Whelps* was take into the Royal Navy and the estate reimbursed £4,500 according to Captain Penington who had supervised their construction. Had the fleet been sold to England, as the Earl of Nottingham had done with his *Lion's Whelp* in 1602, very likely much more money would have accrued to the Buckingham estate.

- Buckingham's first *Lion's Whelp* was built by William Castell of Southwark St Saviour in 1628. After the Duke was assassinated in 1632, she was taken into the Royal Navy and then converted into a chain ship for the Chatham "barricado" c. 1641. She was sent to Harwich as a careening hulk in August 1650, and then drops out of the historical record. *Lion's Whelp* may be the hulk at Harwich that was ordered to be sold in October 1651.
- The second *Lion's Whelp* was also built by William Castell of St. Savior's in Southwark. She was converted into a chain ship for the Chatham 'barricado' c.1641, then was

ordered to be sold in August, 1650 together with the *Defiance* and *Merhonour* as having become too decayed, even to be a careening hulk at Harwich.

- The third *Lion's Whelp* was built by John Dearsley of Ipswich at Wapping. She was listed as unfit for service in Batten's survey of 1647 and 'cast' before February, 1643.
- The fourth *Lion's Whelp* was built by Christopher Malim of Redriff. She was used for experimental constructions in the Project Dutchman, c.1633. These works in the hold were ordered for removal in March 1643 because they were of no use in a man-o-war. Details of the experimental constructions are lacking, although Warrell's research points to Cornelius Drebbel as having executed the removal order. The fourth *Lion's Whelp* struck a rock in St. Aubrey's Bay, Jersey on August 4, 1636 and sank without any loss of life.
- The fifth *Lion's Whelp* was built by Peter Marsh of Wapping and spent most of her life in service in Ireland. She foundered in the North Sea on June 28, 1637 and sank with the loss of 17 men. Cause of this tragedy was placed with the shipyard who built her of 'mean, sappy timbers'.
- The sixth *Lion's Whelp* was built by Peter Pett of Ratcliffe. Peter Pett (1610-?1672) was an English Master Shipwright, the second Resident Commissioner of the Chatham Dockyard. Phinaes Pett was viewed as the greatest shipbuilder of his time, indeed perhaps the finest to have ever lived and worked in England. The reputation of the Pett dynasty ensured that the sixth *Lion's Whelp* was designed and constructed to the highest standards. Her captain was John Pett (1601/2 - 1628), the eldest son of Phineas Pett who died when the ship went down off the coast of Brittany when returning from the La Rochelle expedition in 1628.
- The seventh *Lion's Whelp* was built by Matthew Graves of

Limehouse, She and the famous ship-of-the-line' *Mary Rose* got into a dispute with a Dutch warship from Enkhuisen over a Dutch privateer captured off the Suffolk coast. Negligence in the powder store led to a fierce explosion that destroyed the seventh *Lion's Whelp* amidst action involving several ships from both countries. There is speculation that Captain Cooper became severely disoriented immediately after the loss of the ship, and thereafter was mentally incompetent.

- The eighth *Lion's Whelp* was built in the yard of John Graves of Limehouse. In 1633 she was given to George Cateret as his first independent command. His first task was to attend the Vauntguard which Penington commanded (Balleine, op. cit, p10). Later, in 1644 she was used to transport gold to the Scottish parliament. The Eighth is another pinnace in the Duke's fleet that went 'rotten'. In July 1645, she was judged too decayed to repair and ordered to be laid up on the Woolwich shore.
- The ninth *Lion's Whelp* was also built by John Graves of Limehouse and spent her active years in the Irish service. Her captain was Dawtrey Cooper in 1632/33, who had been the captain of the seventh *Lion's Whelp* when a seaman's negligence caused a fearful explosion and loss of life. During the ninth *Lion's Whelp* service at Ireland, there were continual disputes and near mutinies. She came to an end as a wreck in the River Clyde with the pinnace *Confidence* while taking supplies from Ireland to Dumbarton Castle (which is on the Clyde near Glasgow) in April, 1640. There is an incorrect record that the eighth and ninth *Lion's Whelps* were lost in a storm in 1628 that had wrecked the sixth. After a brief period of out of contact, the eighth and ninth returned to Portsmouth.
- The tenth *Lion's Whelp* was built by Robert Tranckmore of Shoreham, went over to the Royalists after the fall of Bristol in 1643, then was recaptured by Parliament's

forces in 1645. She was at Helvoetsluys with the Earl of Warwick's fleet in 1648, then was fitted out as a fireship for Blake's pursuit of Prince Rupert to Lisbon in 1650. Later the tenth *Lion's Whelp* was used for convoy work and communications during the First Anglo-Dutch War. The last historical mention of the tenth *Lion's Whelp* is on October 19, 1654 when she was sold to Jacob Blackpath for £410.

With sale of the tenth, this fleet of *Lion's Whelps* passes from recorded history. Their fragmentary historical record has provided additional information about the building of small war ships in the 17th century, and activities of the Royal Navy in the Anglo-French War.

Upwey, Dorset

[Editor's Note: Upwey, England is the place of origin for most the original Sprague's that travelled to America in the 17th century.]

Upwey is a suburb of Weymouth in south Dorset, England. The suburb is situated on the B3159 road in the Wey valley. The area was formerly a village until it was absorbed into the Weymouth built-up area. It is located four miles north of the town centre in the outer suburbs. During the Census 2001 the combined population of Upwey and neighbouring Broadwey was 4,349.

The village has a 13th-century parish church, dedicated to Saint Lawrence, and a manor house, Upwey Manor, which was owned by the Gould family. A disc barrow is located above the village on the Ridgeway at map reference SY 663866.

The River Wey rises at the foot of the chalk ridge of the South Dorset Downs, which rise above Upwey to the north, and flows through the village. The source is known as the Upwey Wishing Well and was a tourist attraction as far back as the Victorian era. There is now a tea room at the site, complete with mature water gardens. In the 18th century a water mill was built on the river, rebuilt in 1802; it featured in Thomas Hardy's *The Trumpet Major*; he also wrote a poem "At the Railway Station, Upway", which most likely relates to Upwey station. Another famous name associated with Upwey is that of Lucille Ball the American actress, comedian who was proud of her family and heritage. Her genealogy can be traced back to the earliest settlers in the colonies. One direct ancestor, William Sprague (1609–1675), left England on the ship Lyon's Whelp for Plymouth/Salem, Massachusetts. They were from Upwey, Dorset, England. Along with his two brothers,

William helped to found the city of Charlestown, Massachusetts. Other Sprague relatives became soldiers in the US Revolutionary War and two of them became governors of the state of Rhode Island.

Upwey lends its name to Upwey, Victoria, in Melbourne, Australia, near Belgrave, Victoria.

Upwey, England Scrapbook

THE OLD SHIP INN

Former Methodist chapel

13th Century Church of St Laurence - Upwey

Upwey Wishing Well Halt in 1939 with a double-headed train coming up the incline from the Weymouth direction and travelling towards the Bincombe Tunnel and Dorchester beyond. Modified after a photograph taken from the road bridge near the hairpin bend on the Dorchester Road at Upwey by the late Ray Tustin in 1939. Ian West, 2009.

Upwey Wishing Well, Dorset

Online Copy Protection. © The Francis Frith Collection

Sprague Miscellany

The Steamer *Sprague*

"*The Big Mama of the Mississippi*"

The largest and most powerful stern wheel towboat ever launched (318 feet long, 61 feet wide), the steamer Sprague, was constructed in 1901 by the Dubuque Boat and Boiler Works in Iowa for the Monongehela River Consolidated Coal and Coke Company. The Sprague broke the record for towing when, in 1907, it pushed the largest tow of barges handled by a steam-powered vessel- 60 units, 1,125 feet long, 312 feet

wide, and 67,307 tons. Unfortunately it also broke the record for the most tows lost- 53,200 tons of coal above Osceola, Arkansas.
In April 1927, the steamer transported human cargo during the massive Mississippi River flood, rescuing an estimated 20,000 people bringing them to Vicksburg.

In 1948, the steamboat was decommissioned at Memphis having traveled a distance equal to forty times around the equator and was to be scraped. A reprieve came from the citizens of Vicksburg who purchased the Sprague for use as a floating theater for the melodrama Gold in the Hills and as the home of a river-related museum and the Vicksburg Yacht Club.

Affectionately called "Big Mama," the Sprague burned in 1974 and eventually sank in 1979.

Sprague High School

Charles A. Sprague High School, known as Sprague High School, is a high school in the Sunnyslope neighborhood of Salem, Oregon, United States. The school is named after Charles A. Sprague, who served as Oregon's governor from 1939 to 1943.

USS Clifton Sprague (FFG-16)

USS *Clifton Sprague*, 17 November 1980

Name:	USS *Clifton Sprague*
Namesake:	Vice Admiral Clifton A. F. Sprague
Ordered:	27 February 1976
Builder:	Bath Iron Works
Laid down:	30 July 1979
Launched:	16 February 1980
Sponsored by:	Courtney Sprague Vaughan, daughter of Adm. Sprague
Commissioned:	21 March 1981
Decommissioned:	2 June 1995
Struck:	4 September 1997

Homeport:	Naval Station Mayport
Identification:	Hull symbol:FFG-16
Motto:	"Nunc Paratus" (Ready Now)
Fate:	Disposed of through the Security Assistance Program (SAP)
Career (Turkey)	
Name:	TCG *Gaziantep*
Namesake:	Gaziantep
Acquired:	27 August 1997
Identification:	(F 490)
Status:	in active service, as of 2015
General characteristics	
Class and type:	*Oliver Hazard Perry*-class frigate
Displacement:	4,100 long tons (4,200 t), full load
Length:	445 feet (136 m), overall
Beam:	45 feet (14 m)
Draft:	22 feet (6.7 m)
Propulsion:	2 × General Electric LM2500-30 gas turbines generating 41,000 shp (31 MW) through a single shaft and variable pitch propeller 2 × Auxiliary Propulsion Units, 350 hp (260 kW) retractable electric azimuth thrusters for maneuvering and docking.
Speed:	over 29 knots (54 km/h)
Range:	5,000 nautical miles at 18 knots (9,300 km at 33 km/h)
Complement:	15 officers and 190 enlisted, plus SH-60 LAMPS detachment of roughly six officer pilots and 15 enlisted maintainers

Sensors and processing systems:	AN/SPS-49 air-search radar AN/SPS-55 surface-search radar CAS and STIR fire-control radar AN/SQS-56 sonar.
Electronic warfare and decoys:	AN/SLQ-32
Armament:	**As built:** 1 × OTO Melara Mk 75 76 mm/62 caliber naval gun 2 × Mk 32 triple-tube (324 mm) launchers for Mark 46 torpedoes 1 × Vulcan Phalanx CIWS; four .50-cal (12.7 mm) machine guns. 1 × Mk 13 Mod 4 single-arm launcher for Harpoon anti-ship missiles and SM-1MR Standard anti-ship/air missiles (40 round magazine) **Note:** As of 2004, Mk 13 systems removed from all active US vessels of this class.
Aircraft carried:	1 × SH-2F LAMPS I helicopter[1]

USS *Clifton Sprague* (FFG-16), is an *Oliver Hazard Perry*-class guided missile frigate of the United States Navy, the tenth ship of that class. She was named for Vice Admiral Clifton A.

F. Sprague (1896–1955), hero of the Samar action of the Battle of Leyte Gulf, where he received the Navy Cross. *Clifton Sprague* (FFG-16) was the first ship of that name in the US Navy.

History

Ordered from Bath Iron Works on 27 February 1976 as part of the FY76 program, *Clifton Sprague* was laid down 30 July 1979, launched 16 February 1980, and commissioned 21 March 1981. *Clifton Sprague* was part of the forces during Operation Urgent Fury, the US led 1983 Invasion of Grenada.

In July 1993, the guided-missile cruiser USS *Gettysburg* and *Clifton Sprague* participated in a passing exercise (PASSEX) with three Russian ships, cruiser *Marshal Ustinov*, destroyer *Admiral Kharlamov* and the replenishment ship *Dnester*. This was noteworthy because the two navies had an adversarial relationship for decades prior to the Dissolution of the Soviet Union.

Clifton Sprague was part of the flotilla for Operation Uphold Democracy, the September 1995 US intervention in Haiti.

She was decommissioned on 2 June 1995 at Naval Station Mayport, Florida, and was stricken from the US Navy register on 4 September 1997 after being transferred to Turkey.

TCG *Gaziantep* (F 490)

She was transferred to Turkey on 27 August 1997 as that nation's TCG *Gaziantep* (F 490), and then immediately modified into a G-class frigate by the Turkish Naval Yard. As of 2011, she was still in active service.

Camp Sprague

Photo of Officers of lst Rhode Island Volunteers - Camp Sprague, 1861. It was made between 1861 and 1865.

Howard Sprague

Character from the Andy Griffith Show. Just for fun.

The Sprague Project Website

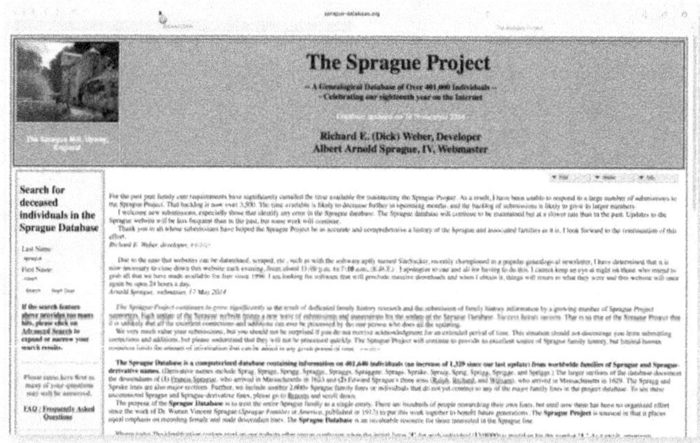

The Sprague Project: A website containing a massive amount of genealogical data pertaining to Spragues.

Genealogy

People List

The following is an alphabetical list of all Spragues that show up in my family tree records. The current, living, generation of names have been removed (as is the practice of most genealogy sites). Naturally, the farther back in time you go, the more likely that these people also appear in your Sprague family tree. The list is presented here to assist you with finding new people or lines in your own research.

Name	Birth	Death
Sprague, Abigail	23 Nov 1729 - Lebanon, New London, Connecticut	14 Oct 1802 - Pomfret, Windham, Connecticut
Sprague, Abigail	23 Feb 1747 - Smithfield, Providence, Rhode Island, United States	-
Sprague, Abigal	12 Mar 1750 - Kent, Litchfield, Connecticut, United States	-
Sprague, Abijah	1772 - Kent, Litchfield Co. CT	8 Feb 1830
Sprague, Albert	9 Nov 1820	1907
Sprague, Alexander	28 Oct 1763 - Kent, Litchfield, Connecticut, United States	1839 - Otsego, Otsego, New York, United States
Sprague, Alexander	28 Oct 1763 - Kent, Litchfield, Connecticut, United States	1839 - Otsego, Otsego, New York, United States
Sprague, Alfred D	1785 - Maine, United States	1840 - Campbell, Kentucky, United States
Sprague, Alice	1596 - Upway, Dorset, England	1668 - Tincleton, England
Sprague, Alice	Abt. Dec 08, 1859 - Michigan	Dec 30, 1933 - Council Bluffs, Pottawattamie County, Iowa
Sprague, Alice H.	8 Dec 1859 - MI	30 Dec 1933 - Council Bluffs, Pottawattamie Co.

		IA
Sprague, Alvah J	5 Oct 1822 - Chautauqua, Chautauqua, New York, United States	9 Mar 1883 - Marionville, Lawrence, Missouri, United States
Sprague, Amasa	29 Mar 1789 - Kent, Litchfield, Connecticut, United States	9 Oct 1846 - Marcellus, Onondaga, New York, United States
Sprague, Ambrose Dennis	1804 - Maine, United States	31 Oct 1874 - Magoffin, Kentucky, United States
Sprague, Amy	1765-04-18 - Greenwich,Washington,New York,USA	1828-09-10
Sprague, Ann	25 Jul 1807 - , Athens, Ohio, USA	6 Oct 1878 - Memphis, Shelby, Tennessee, United States
Sprague, Ann	9 MAR 1709 - Smithfield, Providence, Rhode Island	-
Sprague, Ann Eliza	1841 - Pomfret, Chautauqua, New York	1892 - Chautauqua, New York
SPRAGUE, Anna	27 Jul 1785 - Cumberland, Providence, Ri	19 Dec 1787 - Cumberland, Providence, Rhode Island, United States
Sprague, Anna	1 Apr 1644 - London, London, England	1669 - Duxbury, Plymouth, Massachusetts, United States
sprague, anne	1614 - Plymouth, Plymouth, Massachusetts, United States	1668 - Duxbury, Plymouth, Massachusetts, United States
Sprague, Anne	11 Jan 1728 - Smithfield, Providence, Rhode Island, United States	-
Sprague, Anne	1595	25 Dec 1611 - England
Sprague, Anthony William	2 Sep 1635 - Charlestown, Suffolk, Massachusetts, United States	3 Sep 1719 - Hingham, Plymouth, Massachusetts, United States
Sprague, Arthur G.	abt 1862 - Michigan	Unknown
Sprague, Asa	10 Dec 1761	-
Sprague, Aurilla J	12 Jan 1805 - Northeast, Dutchess, New York, United States	27 May 1885 - Saratoga, Saratoga, New York, United States
Sprague, Barnabas	24 Mar 1723 - New London, New London, Connecticut, United States	10 Apr 1724 - New London, New London, Connecticut, United States
Sprague, Benjamin	23 Mar 1722 - Lebanon, New London, Connecticut, USA	17 Jun 1723 - Lebanon, New London, Connecticut,

		USA
Sprague, Benjamin	7 Nov 1757 - Kent, Litchfield, Connecticut	abt 1830 - Buckland, Franklin, Massachusetts
Sprague, Benjamin	25 Mar 1753 - Kent, Litchfield, Connecticut, United States	-
SPRAGUE, Benjami n	15 Jul 1686 - Duxbury, Plymouth, Massachusetts, United States	15 Jul 1754 - Lebanon, New London, Connecticut, United States
Sprague, Benjamin	8 Mar 1740 - Lebanon, New London, Connecticut, United States	5 Sep 1772 - Smith, Belmont, Ohio, United States
Sprague, Benjamin	5 Jun 1725 - Lebanon, New London, Connecticut, USA	4 Sep 1772 - Kent, Litchfield, Connecticut, USA
SPRAGUE, Benjami n	03 Apr 1778 - Smithfield, Rhode Island, USA	03 Jan 1858 - Fredonia, Chautauqua Co., NY
Sprague, Benjamin	7 May 1813 - Chautauqua, Chautauqua, New York, United States	22 Dec 1879 - Colorado Springs, El Paso, Colorado, United States
Sprague, Bernard	Jun 1897 - Michigan	-
Sprague, Bernard E	12 Jun 1897 - Michigan	06/30/1959 - Ann Arbor, Michigan, USA
Sprague, Bert	Jun 1888 - Michigan	-
Sprague, Bert E	21 Jun 1888 - Michigan,United States of America	-
Sprague, Bertha S.	abt 1871 - Kansas	1939 - Saline, Washtenaw, Michigan, USA
SPRAGUE, Bethiah	24 MAY 1707 - Smithfield, Providence, Rhode Island	-
Sprague, Carrie	May 1870 - Michigan	-
Sprague, Carrie E.	abt 1862 - New York	-
Sprague, Chauncy	24 Aug 1823 - New York	1869
Sprague, Christoph er	1607 - Upwey, Dorset, England	21 March 1625 - Dorset, England
Sprague, Christop her	1571	1678
Sprague, Clarence H.	abt 1874 - Kansas	1952

Sprague, Dean Patrick	Dec 14, 1992 - Sacramento, California, USA	-
Sprague, Deborah	21 Sep 1670 - Malden, Middlesex, Massachusetts, United States	17 Aug 1751 - Malden, Middlesex, Massachusetts, United States
SPRAGUE, Debor ah	1665 - Duxbury, Plymouth, Massachusetts, United States	10 Jan 1709 - Falmouth, Plymouth, Massachusetts, United States
SPRAGUE, Debor ah	09 Dec 1775 - Cumberland, Providence, Ri	02 Nov 1844
Sprague, Desire	1665 - Duxbury, Plymouth, Massachusetts, United States	1700 - Rochester, Plymouth, Massachusetts, United States
Sprague, Donald E	abt 1925 - Michigan	-
Sprague, Dorcas	1666 - Duxbury, Plymouth, Massachusetts, United States	10 Jan 1710 - Duxbury, Plymouth, Massachusetts, United States
Sprague, Dorcas	1635 - Duxbury, Plymouth, Massachusetts, USA	1716 - Dartmouth, Bristol, Massachusetts, USA
Sprague, Dorothy	6 Oct 1599 - Piddletown, Dorset, , England	Feb 1663 - Piddletown, Dorset, , England
Sprague, Dorothy Beatrice	27 Dec 1901 - Los Angeles Co. CA	9 Mar 1984 - Los Angeles Co. CA
Sprague, Ebeneze r	4 Dec 1800 - Cooperstown, Otsego, New York, United States	-
Sprague, Ebeneze r	1705 - Lebanon, New London, Massachusetts, United States	1771 - Sharon, Litchfield, Connecticut, United States
Sprague, Ebeneze r	20 Oct 1768	5 Mar 1772 - Kent, Litchfield, Connecticut, United States
Sprague, Edward	5 Jan 1576 - Upway, Dorset, England	6 Jun 1614 - Upway, Dorset, England
Sprague, Edward	1663 - Malden, Middlesex, Massachusetts, United States	13 Apr 1715 - Malden, Middlesex, Massachusetts, United States
Sprague, Edward	15 December 1601 - Dorset, England	15 December 1633 - Upwey, Dorset, England
Sprague, Edward	15 December 1601 - Dorset, England	15 December 1633 - Upwey, Dorset, England
Sprague, Edward	1854	1856

A

Sprague, Edward Jr	15 Dec 1601 - Upway, Dorset, England	25 Nov 1668 - New England
SPRAGUE, Eliakim	10 Oct 1711 - Lebanon, New London, Connecticut, USA	10 Dec 1786 - Coventry, Tolland, Connecticut, USA
Sprague, Elise E	Jul 1892 - Michigan	-
SPRAGUE, Elizabeth	2 May 1641 - Hingham, Plymouth, Massachusetts, United States	1647 - Hingham, Plymouth, Massachusetts, United States
Sprague, Elizabeth	8 May 1589 - Piddletown, Dorset, , England	30 Oct 1632 - Piddletown, Dorset, , England
Sprague, Elizabeth	21 Jul 1670	1752
Sprague, Elizabeth	1657 - Duxbury, Plymouth, Massachusetts, United States	27 May 1727 - Plympton, Plymouth, Massachusetts, United States
Sprague, Elkanah	25 Jan 1731 - Lebanon, New London, Connecticut, United States	1805 - Hartford, Windsor, Vermont, United States
Sprague, Elliot Harroun	26 Apr 1861	12 Jul 1863
Sprague, Elmer H.	26 Oct 1863 - Rives Junction, Jackson Co. MI	15 Sep 1935 - Covina, Los Angeles Co, CA
Sprague, Elmer H.	Apr 1864 - Michigan	-
Sprague, Elnora	Jan 1848 - Schroeppel, Oswego Co. NY	1924
Sprague, Elverton	16 Mar 1852 - Oswego Co. NY	10 Apr 1852 - Oswego Co. NY
Sprague, Enos Hugh	1525 - , Dorset, , England	1554 - St George, Dorset, , England
Sprague, Ephraim	15 Mar 1684 - Duxbury, Plymouth, Massachusetts, United States	1763 - Lebanon, New London, Connecticut, United States
Sprague, Ester	3 Mar 1737 - Lebanon, New London, Connecticut, United States	-
Sprague, Eudora	10 May 1850 - Oswego Co.	10 Mar 1851 - Oswego Co.

	NY	NY
Sprague, Eunice	16 Feb 1756	-
Sprague, Eva A	Oct 1865 - Michigan	Apr 23, 1923 - Belleville, Essex County, New Jersey
Sprague, Evangel S.	22 July 1876 - Washington, Kansas, United States	2 May 1945 - Council Bluffs, Pottawattamie, Iowa, United States
Sprague, Fanny	22 Mar 1788	2 Dec 1840 - Smyma, Chenango Co., NY
Sprague, Francis	1590 - London, Greater London, England	2 Mar 1679 - Duxbury, Plymouth County, Massachusetts, United States of America
Sprague, Francis	1620	-
Sprague, Freelove	24 Mar 1723 - Lebanon, New London, Connecticut	6 Oct 1722 - Lebanon, New London, Connecticut
Sprague, Genevive	Nov 14, 1868 - Rives Junction, Jackson County, Michigan	Unknown
Sprague, George Bradley	1848 - Fredonia, Chautauqua, New York	1848 - Fredonia, Chautauqua, New York
Sprague, George Milton	25 Aug 1836 - New York	Mar 06, 1927 - State Hospital at Clarinda, Page Co. IA
Sprague, Glen A	abt 1923 - Michigan	-
Sprague, Grace	30 Oct 1591 - Piddletown, Dorset, , England	Feb 1663 - Piddleton, Dorset, , England
Sprague, Guthrie	04 Mar 1853 - Schroeppel, Oswego Co. NY	Abt. 17 Oct 1898 - Syracuse, Onondaga Co. NY
Sprague, H. Sophia	Unknown	Unknown
Sprague, Haddassah	2 Jun 1732 - Smithfield, Providence, Rhode Island, United States	1788
Sprague, Hannah	25 Feb 1654 - New Plymouth Col, Plymouth, Massachusetts, USA	31 Mar 1658 - Hingham, Plymouth, Massachusetts, USA
Sprague, Hannah	12 Sep 1583 - Puddletown, Dorset, Massachusetts, USA	25 Dec 1611 - Dorchester, Dorset, , England
Sprague, Harley J.	Mar 1867 - Michigan	Abt. 1932 - St. Clair County, Michigan

Sprague, Harold W	abt 1927 - Michigan	-
Sprague, Helen Sabina	25 Oct 1845 - Chautauqua, New York, USA	22 Mar 1884 - Fredonia, Chautauqua, New York, USA
SPRAGUE, Henry	22 Nov 1769 - Smithfield, Providence, Ri	31 Oct 1791
Sprague, Henry Horace	Dec 29, 1857 - Rives Junction, Jackson County, Michigan	18 Jun 1932 - Almena, Norton, Kansas, United States
Sprague, Henry James	1858 - New York	9 Nov 1889 - Cook, Illinois, United States
Sprague, Heny	abt 1859 - New York	-
Sprague, Hezekiah	14 Jul 1737 - Smithfield, Providence, Rhode Island, United States	1793 - Smithfield, Providence, Rhode Island, United States
SPRAGUE, Hezekial	12 Jan 1703 - Smithfield, Providence, Rhode Island, USA	May 1785 - Smithfield, Providence, Rhode Island, USA
Sprague, Hiram	01 Dec 1844 - Onondaga Co. NY	04 Feb 1845 - Onondaga Co. NY
Sprague, Hiram Christopher	21 May 1840 - NY State	Oct 1925 - Eaton Rapids, Eaton Co. MI
SPRAGUE, Hudassa	26 Aug 1773 - Cumberland, Providence, Ri	27 Jul 1836 - Providence, Providence, Rhode Island, United States
Sprague, Irene	1697 - Duxbury, Plymouth, Massachusetts, United States	1729
SPRAGUE, James	07 Jun 1780 - Cumberland, Providence, Ri	1804 - Chautauqua, Chautauqua, New York, United States
Sprague, James Benjamin	26 Sep 1817 - Pomfret, Chautauqua, New York, United States	4 Aug 1887 - Fredonia, Chautauqua, New York, USA
Sprague, Jenny F.	14 Nov 1868 - Michigan	-
Sprague, Jerusha	20 Oct 1720 - Lebanon, New London, Connecticut, USA	1795 - Tupperville, , Nova Scotia, Canada
Sprague, Joanna	1676 - Richmond, Washington, Rhode Island, United States	22 Dec 1757 - South Kingstown, Washington, Rhode Island, United States
Sprague, Joanna	16 Dec 1644 - Hingham, Plymouth, Massachusetts, United States	11 Jul 1678 - Watertown, Middlesex, Massachusetts, United States

Sprague, Johan	1501 - Upway, Dorset, England	1526 - Upway, Dorset, England
Sprague, JOHN	23 May 1624 - St George, Dorset, England	26 Oct 1683 - Malden,Middlesex,Massachusetts,USA
Sprague, John	1638 - Hingham, Plymouth, Massachusetts, United States	1639
Sprague, John	ABT APR 1638	26 OCT 1683 - Mendon, Massachusetts
Sprague, John	2 Apr 1727 - Providence, Providence, Rhode Island, USA	1776 - Richmond, Ontario, New York, United States
Sprague, John Jr	1656 - Duxbury, Plymouth, Massachusetts, United States	6 Mar 1728 - Lebanon, New London, Connecticut, United States
Sprague, John	5 Sep 1709 - Lebanon, Windham, Connecticut, USA	5 Feb 1777 - Andover, Tolland, Connecticut, USA
Sprague, John	26 Mar 1603 - Duxbury, Plymouth, Massachusetts, USA	26 Mar 1676 - Swampfight, King Phillip War, Massachusetts, United States
Sprague, John	1656 - Duxbury, Plymouth, Massachusetts, United States	6 Mar 1728 - Lebanon, New London, Connecticut, United States
Sprague, John	12 Mar 1749 - Kent, Litchfield, Connecticut, United States	23 Dec 1839 - Sayrna, New York, United States
Sprague, John	1785	10 Mar 1866
Sprague, John Francis	26 Mar 1633 - Duxbury, Plymouth, Massachusetts, USA	26 Mar 1676 - Pawtucket, Providence County, Rhode Island, United States of America
Sprague, Jonathan	22 Apr 1672 - Smithfield, Providence, Rhode Island, United States	22 Apr 1764 - Smithfield, Providence, Rhode Island, United States
SPRAGUE, Jonathan	25 JUL 1701 - Providence, Providence, Rhode Island	1779 - Cumberland, Providence, Rhode Island
SPRAGUE, Jonathan	20 Mar 1642 - New Plymouth Col, Plymouth, Massachusetts, United States	4 Jul 1647 - Hingham, Plymouth, Massachusetts, United States
Sprague, Jonathan	28 May 1648 - Hingham, Plymouth, Massachusetts, USA	10 Apr 1756 - Smithfield, Providence, Rhode Island, USA
SPRAGUE, Joseph	27 Aug 1771 - Smithfield, Providence, Ri	-

Sprague, Joseph	15 Jan 1739 - Smithfield, Providence, Rhode Island, United States	Sep 1808 - Butternuts, Otsego, New York, USA
Sprague, Joseph	27 Aug 1771 - Smithfield, Providence, Rhode Island, United States	Apr 1837 - Wooster, Wayne, Ohio, United States
Sprague, joseph	1635	-
Sprague, Joseph Jilson	8 May 1811 - Pomfret, Chautauqua, New York, United States	2 Mar 1890 - Cassadaga, Chautauqua, New York, United States
Sprague, Julia Ann	31 Jan 1809 - Zanesville, Muskingum, Ohio, United States	5 Mar 1874 - Du Quoin, Perry, Illinois, United States
Sprague, Lewis Guthrie	31 Aug 1818 - Chenango Co. NY	1903 - Schroeppel, Oswego Co. NY
Sprague, Lindsay Erin	Dec 14, 1992 - Sacramento, California, USA	-
Sprague, Lois	7 Feb 1754 - Kent, Litchfield, Connecticut, United States	-
Sprague, Lois M.	abt 1865 - Michigan	Unknown
Sprague, Louisa Abigail	May 10, 1833 - New York	11 Sep 1918 - Lansing, Ingham Co. MI
Sprague, Louisa S.	27 Apr 1815 - Chenango Co. NY	12 Mar 1828 - Chenango Co. NY
Sprague, Lydia	19 Nov 1757 - Kent, Litchfield, Connecticut, USA	5 Feb 1831 - Russia, Herkimer, New York, United States
Sprague, Lydia	20 Mar 1735 - Lebanon, New London, Connecticut	-
Sprague, Lydia	1692 - Duxbury, Plymouth, Massachusetts, United States	3 Mar 1762 - Sharon, Litchfield, Connecticut, United States
Sprague, Lydia	20 Feb 1726 - Smithfield, Providence, Rhode Island, USA	8 Jul 1821 - New Berlin, Chenango, New York, USA
Sprague, Lyman W	16 Jul 1863 - New York	8 Jan 1890 - Cook, Illinois, United States
Sprague, Marie	1505 - Upway, Dorset, England	England
Sprague, Marion	1896 - Jackson, Jackson Co.	-

L.	MI	
Sprague, Martha	1 May 1593 - Piddletown, Dorsetshire, England, England	25 Dec 1611 - Dorchester, Dorset, England
Sprague, Martha	1852 - Dumbarton, New Brunswick, Canada	-
Sprague, Mary	1624 - St Marys, Dorset, England	-
Sprague, Mary	1 May 1593 - Upway, Dorset, England	-
Sprague, Mary	16 Mar 1624 - Dorchester, Dorset, England	1677 - Charles City, Charles, Virginia, United States
Sprague, Mary	1608 - England	1677 - Charles City, Charles, Virginia, United States
Sprague, Mary	1652-04-25 - Hingham, Plymouth, MA, USA	31 Mar 1658 - Hingham, Plymouth, Massachusetts, USA
Sprague, Mary	1697 - Smithfield, Providence, Rhode Island, United States	29 Aug 1770 - Providence, Providence, Rhode Island, United States
Sprague, Mary	10 Sep 1740 - Lebanon, New London, Connecticut, United States	21 Apr 1806 - Coventry, Tolland, Connecticut, United States
SPRAGUE, Mary	5 Mar 1712 - Lebanon, New London, Connecticut, USA	1754
Sprague, Mary	24 Oct 1765	-
Sprague, Mary Jane	10 Nov 1839 - NY, , Michigan, USA	25 May 1924 - Eaton Rapids, Eaton Co. MI
Sprague, Mary Jane	1842 - Fredonia, Chautauqua, New York	1842 - Fredonia, Chautauqua, New York
Sprague, Mary Maria E	3 Jun 1856 - New York	2 Jun 1878
Sprague, Maryabe th	19 Mar 1710 - Smithfield, Providence, Rhode Island, United States	-
Sprague, Mehitabl e	7 Mar 1735 - Smithfield, Providence, Rhode Island, United States	1766
SPRAGUE, Mehita ble	21 MAR 1711 - Smithfield, Providence, Rhode Island	-

SPRAGUE, Mehitable	14 May 1782 - Cumberland, Providence, Ri	-
Sprague, Mercy	12 Mar 1744 - Smithfield, Providence, Rhode Island, United States	1834 - Smithfield, Providence, Rhode Island, United States
Sprague, Mercy	1623 - Plymouth, Plymouth, Massachusetts, United States	13 Jun 1668 - Duxbury, Plymouth, Massachusetts, United States
Sprague, Milton Amasa	15 Feb 1832 - Oswego, Onondaga, New York, United States	3 Mar 1897 - Los Angeles, Los Angeles, California, United States
Sprague, Minor	5 Mar 1733 - Lebanon, New London, Connecticut, United States	1770 - Taunton, Bristol, Massachusetts, United States
Sprague, Mrs Enos	1525 - Upway,,Dorset,England	Y, Somme, Picardie, France
Sprague, Nancy	1788 - Maine, United States	1 Aug 1853 - China, Kennebec, Maine, United States
Sprague, Olive	27 Sep 1824 - Chautauqua, Chautauqua, New York, United States	20 Dec 1902 - Du Quoin, Perry, Illinois, United States
Sprague, Olive Arminda	18 Jun 1846 - Onondaga Co. NY	24 Sep 1847
Sprague, Patience	1674 - Smithfield, Providence, Rhode Island, United States	29 Aug 1770 - Pawtucket, Providence, Rhode Island, United States
Sprague, Persis	1681 - Smithfield, Providence, Rhode Island, United States	1730
SPRAGUE, Persis	12 Nov 1643 - Hingham, Plymouth, Massachusetts, United States	1684 - Marshfield, Plymouth, Massachusetts, United States
Sprague, Peter	1611 - Upway, Dorset, England	Dorset, England
Sprague, Peter	22 Apr 1771 - Sidney, Kennebec, Maine, United States	Mar 1837 - Gallipolis, Gallia, Ohio, United States
Sprague, Peter	27 Apr 1771 - Kent, Litchfield Co. CT	9 Jul 1809 - Hamilton Center, Madison Co. NY
Sprague, Philip	abt 1929 - New Jersey	-
Sprague, Phineas	Apr 1668 - Malden, Middlesex, Massachusetts, United States	23 Jan 1690 - Malden, Middlesex, Massachusetts, United States

Sprague, Phineas	5 Sep 1717 - Lebanon, New London, Connecticut, USA	5 Feb 1777 - Andover, Tolland, Connecticut, United States
Sprague, Rachel or Hannah	20 NOV 1716 - Smithfield, Providence, Rhode Island	1759 - Richmond, Cheshire, New Hampshire, USA
Sprague, Ralph	20 Jun 1599 - Upway, Dorset, England	24 Nov 1650 - Malden, Essex, Massachusetts, United States
Sprague, Raymond Harris	Aug 26, 1892	Oct 05, 1895
Sprague, Raymond Milton	30 Jul 1866 - Michigan, United States	29 Nov 1899 - California, United States
Sprague, Rebecca	7 Feb 1585 - Piddletown, Dorset, , England	Feb 1663
Sprague, Richard	20 Jun 1604 - Upway, Dorset, , England	25 Nov 1668 - Charlestown, Suffolk, Massachusetts, United States
Sprague, Richmond	1575	15 Apr 1644 - Upway, Dorset, England
Sprague, Robert Gene	13 May 1925 - Michigan	30 Jun 1997 - San Jose, Santa Clara, California, USA
Sprague, Ross C	abt 1927 - New Jersey	-
Sprague, Ross Clifford	21 Oct 1894 - Michigan,United States of America	14 Apr 1942
Sprague, Ross Gilbert	29 Mar 1869 - Jackson, Jackson Co. MI	8 Nov 1919 - Newark, Essex Co. NJ
Sprague, Ruth	12 Feb 1660 - Duxbury, Plymouth, Massachusetts, United States	1743 - Duxbury, Plymouth, Massachusetts, United States
Sprague, Ruth	1693	-
Sprague, Ruth	5 Sep 1704 - New London, New London, Connecticut, United States	1730
Sprague, Ruth	26 Dec 1727 - Smithfield, Providence, Rhode Island, United States	22 Dec 1816
Sprague, Ruth S	Aug 1890 - Michigan	-

Sprague, Samuel	24 May 1640 - Hingham, Plymouth, Massachusetts, USA	1710 - Marshfield, Plymouth, Massachusetts, USA
Sprague, Samuel	31 Dec 1688 - Duxbury, Plymouth, Massachusetts, United States	21 May 1725 - Lebanon, New London, Connecticut, United States
Sprague, Samuel	1662 - Duxbury, Plymouth, Massachusetts, United States	24 Jul 1740 - Hingham, Plymouth, Massachusetts, United States
Sprague, Sarah	Feb 1672 - Malden, Middlesex, Massachusetts, United States	1752
Sprague, Sarah	1644	1722
Sprague, Sarah	8 Nov 1771 - Kent, Litchfield, Connecticut, United States	-
Sprague, Sarah	1 Jan 1760	11 Feb 1761 - Kent, Litchfield, Connecticut, United States
Sprague, Sarah	15 Mar 1742 - Smithfield, Providence, Rhode Island, United States	-
Sprague, Sarah	24 NOV 1761 - Smithfield, Providence Co., Ri	1820 - prob. Providence, Providence Co., Ri
Sprague, Sarah	24 Nov 1761 - Smithfield, Providence, Rhode Island, United States	17 Jan 1820 - Providence, Providence, Rhode Island, United States
Sprague, Sarah	1 Apr 1815 - Chautauqua, Chautauqua, New York, United States	22 Jun 1902 - Du Quoin, Perry, Illinois, United States
Sprague, Silas	20 Jan 1726 - Lebanon, New London, Connecticut	16 Jul 1767 - Lebanon, New London, Connecticut
SPRAGUE, Silas	20 Jan 1726 - Lebanon, New London, Connecticut, United States	Sep 1808 - East Bloomfld, New York, United States
Sprague, Silas	30 Jan 1726 - Lebanon, New London, Connecticut, USA	Sep 1808 - East Bloomfield, Ontario, New York, USA
Sprague, Simon	1550 - Fordington, St George, Dorset, England	26 Jun 1599 - Puddletown, Dorset, , England
Sprague, Stephen	9 Jun 1722 - Providence, Providence, Rhode Island, USA	BEF 11 MAY 1757 - Rhode Island
SPRAGUE, Susan nah	20 Jun 1731 - Providence, Providence, Rhode Island, USA	18 MAR 1821 - Connecticut
Sprague, Susanna h	19 Jan 1809 - Massachusetts, United States	27 Mar 1887 - Gallipolis, Gallia, Ohio, United States

Sprague, Tristram	1550 - Fordingham, St George, Dorset, England	26 Jun 1575 - Dorset, England
Sprague, Verl L	abt 1930 - Michigan	-
Sprague, Verneta J	abt 1934 - Michigan	-
Sprague, William	26 Oct 1609 - Upwales Co, Dorset, England	26 Oct 1675 - Hingham, Plymouth, Massachusetts, United States
Sprague, William	1664 - Duxbury, Plymouth, Massachusetts, United States	25 Nov 1712 - Duxbury, Plymouth, Massachusetts, United States
Sprague, William	-	1821 - Gallipolis, Gallia Ohio
SPRAGUE, William	29 Sep 1715 - Lebanon, New London, Connecticut, USA	9 Apr 1795 - Columbia, Tolland, Connecticut, USA
Sprague, William	9 Jun 1714 - Smithfield, Providence, Rhode Island, USA	16 Jul 1751 - Smithfield, Providence, Rhode Island, USA
Sprague, William	2 Feb 1691 - Smithfield, Providence, RI	20 Oct 1778 - Smithfield, Providence, RI
Sprague, William	23 Apr 1763 - Smithfield, Providence, Rhode Island, United States	1813 - Cooperstown, Otsego, New York, United States
Sprague, William	1578 - Owermoigne, Dorset, , England	15 Apr 1644 - Upway, Dorset, , England
Sprague, William	7 May 1650 - Hingham, Plymouth, Massachusetts, United States	26 Sep 1723 - Providence, Providence, Rhode Island, United States

Family Tree

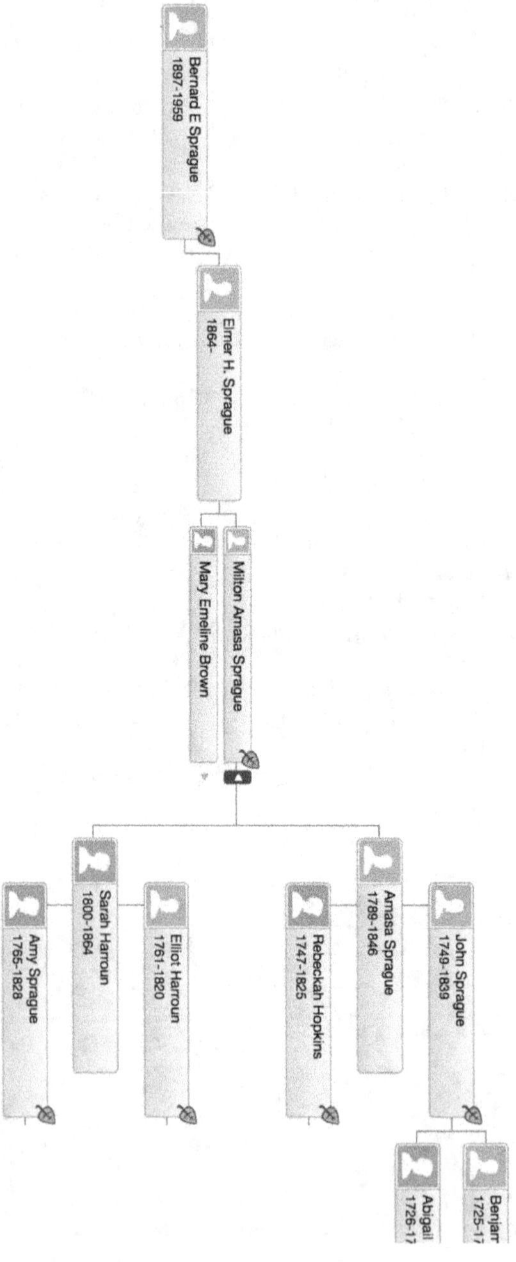

Bernard E Sprague
1897-1959
Elmer H. Sprague
1864-
Milton Amasa Sprague
Mary Emeline Brown
John Sprague
1749-1839
Amasa Sprague
1789-1846
Rebeckah Hopkins
1747-1825
Elliot Harroun
1761-1820
Sarah Harroun
1800-1864
Amy Sprague
1765-1828

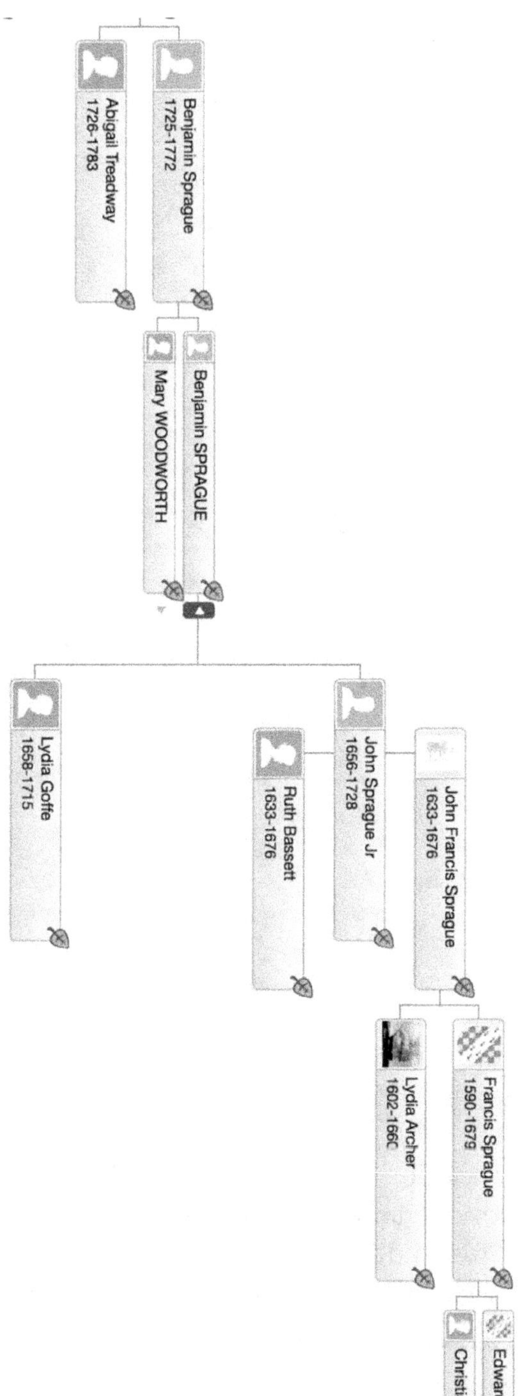

Benjamin Sprague
1725-1772
Abigail Treadway
1726-1783
Benjamin SPRAGUE
Mary WOODWORTH
John Sprague Jr
1656-1728
Lydia Goffe
1658-1715
John Francis Sprague
1633-1676
Ruth Bassett
1633-1676
Francis Sprague
1590-1679
Lydia Archer
Edward
Christian

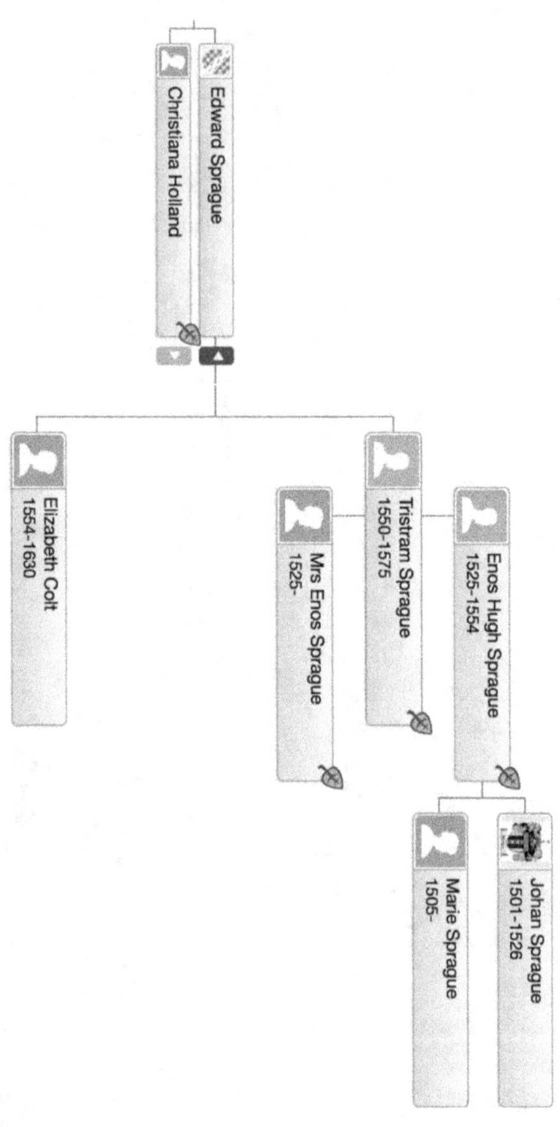

Note: The information in this book should not be used as definitive historical data as it has not been personally verified. However, it is taken directly from the databases of Ancestry.com and FamilySearch.org so it is likely accurate.

Top View:

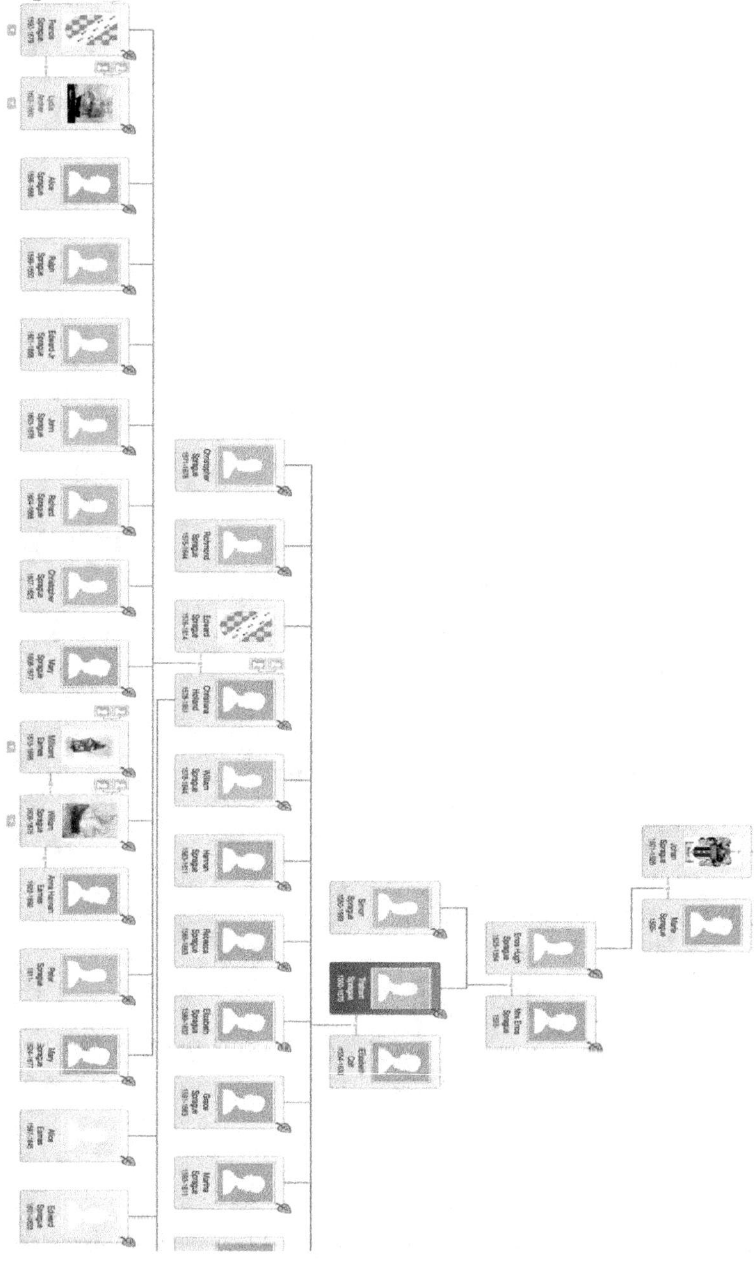

From the William Sprague line:

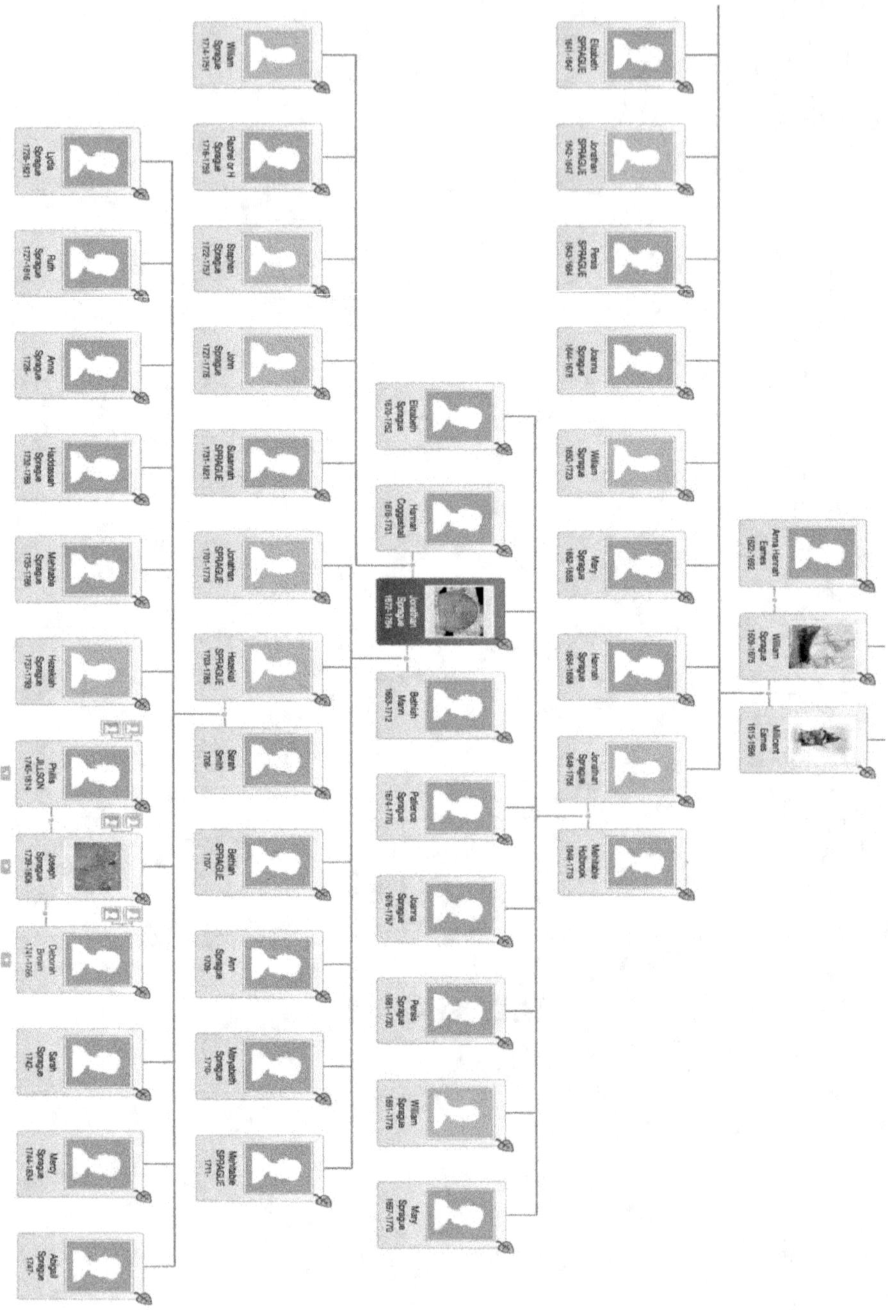

Selections from the Joseph Sprague line:

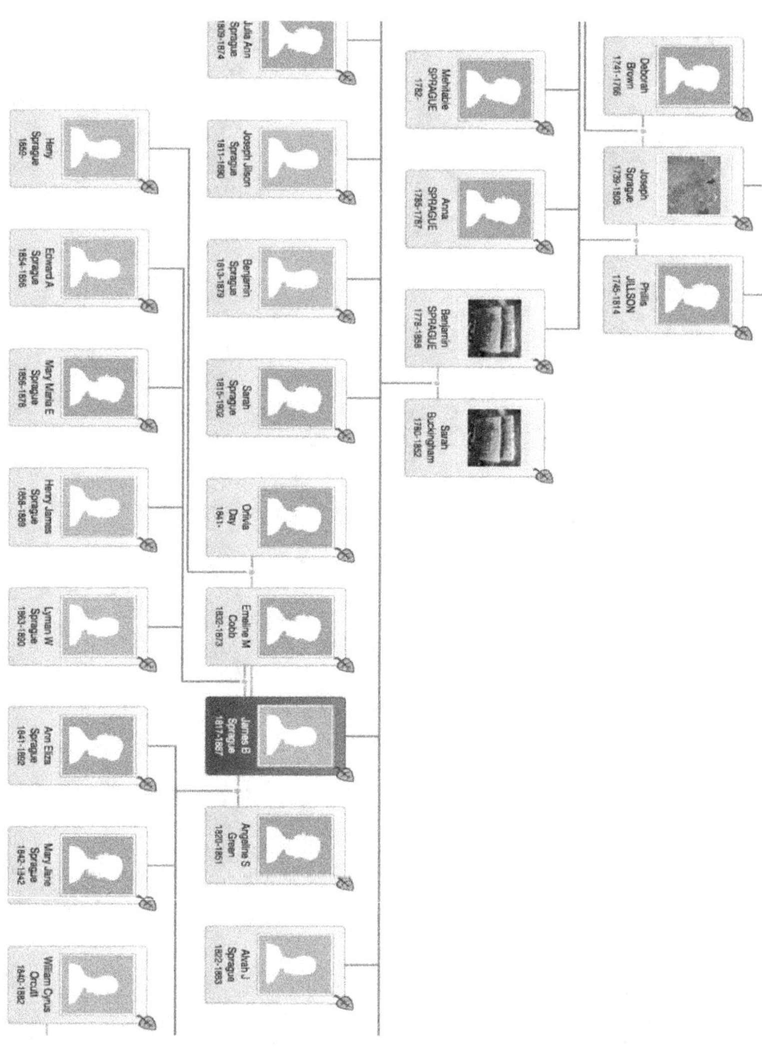

Current Generation Sprague DNA Indicators by Global Region

REGION	APPROXIMATE AMOUNT
Africa	1%
Trace Regions	1%
Cameroon/Congo	1%
Asia	< 1%
Trace Regions	< 1%
Asia South	< 1%
Europe	96%
Europe West	76%
Scandinavia	9%
Trace Regions	11%
Iberian Peninsula	5%
Great Britain	2%
Italy/Greece	2%
Ireland	1%
Europe East	1%
West Asia	2%
Trace Regions	2%
Middle East	< 1%
Caucasus	< 1%

Geographical Distribution in the United States

(Source: http://www.ancestry.com/name-origin?surname=sprague)

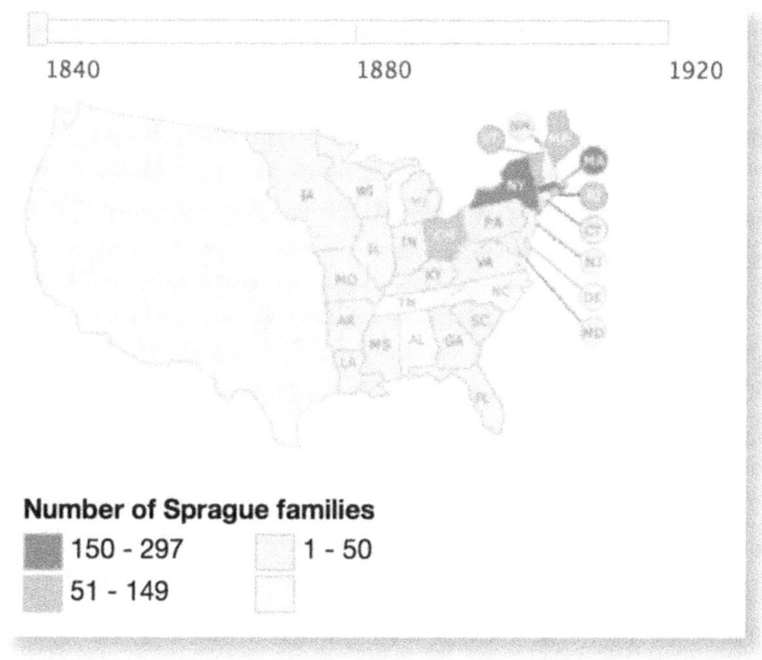

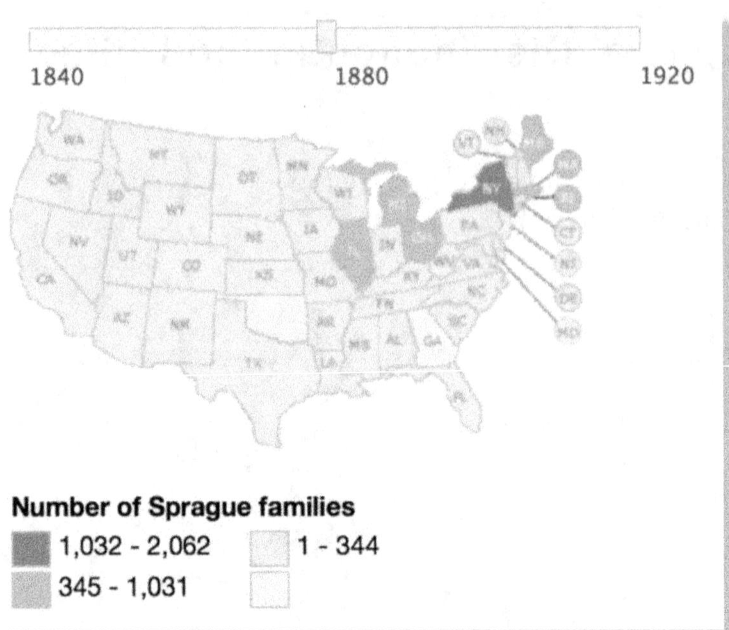
1840
1880
1920
Number of Sprague families
1,032 - 2,062
345 - 1,031
1 - 344

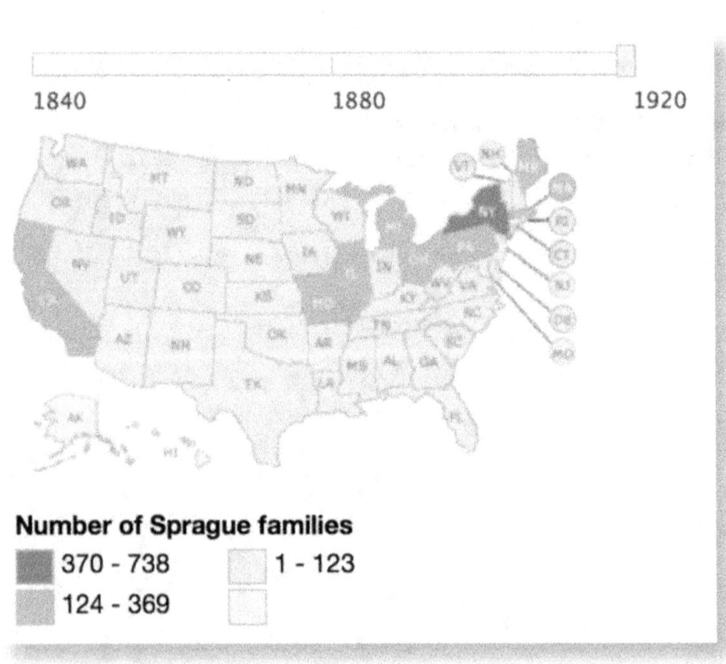
1840
1880
1920
Number of Sprague families
370 - 738
124 - 369
1 - 123

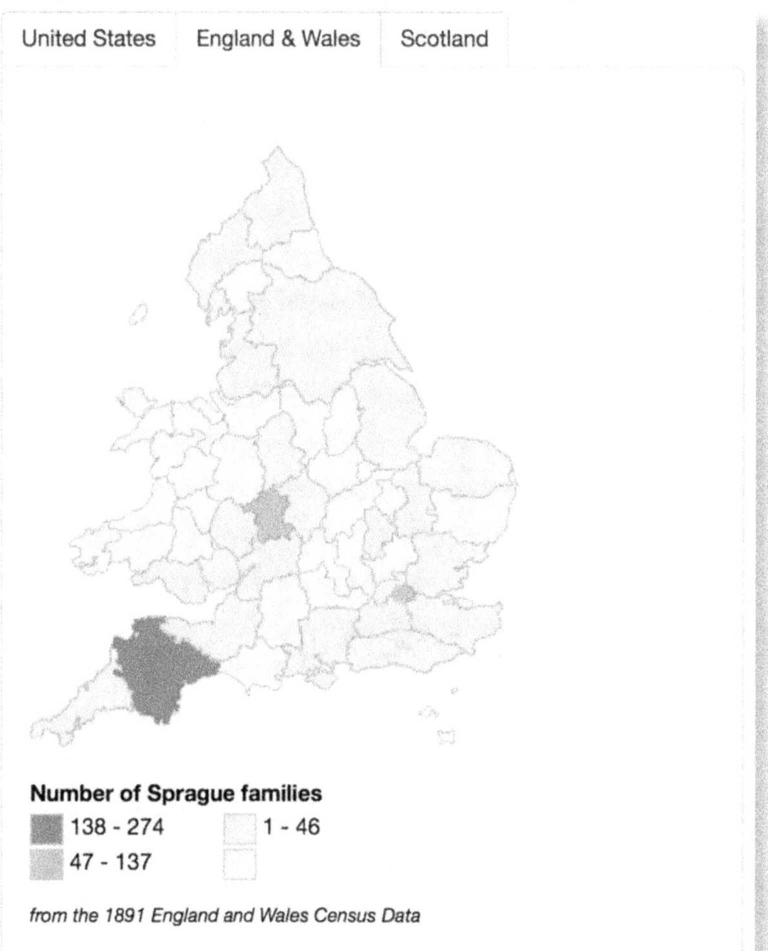
United States
England & Wales
Scotland
Number of Sprague families
138 - 274
47 - 137
1 - 46
from the 1891 England and Wales Census Data

Service in U.S. Civil War

Sprague Civil War Service Records

All Sprague	907
Confederate	23
Union	884

Life Expectancy for Spragues

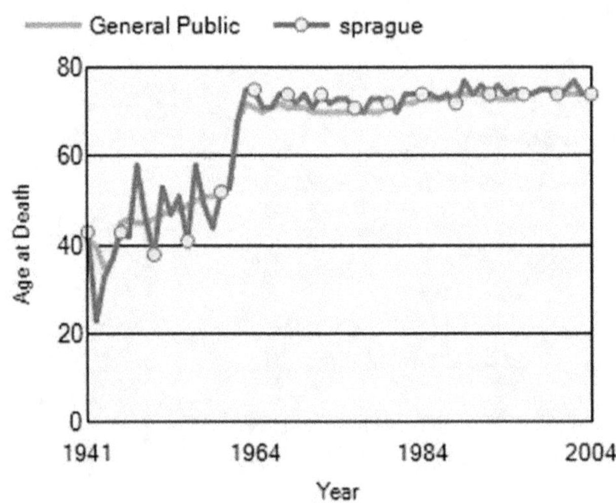

from the *Social Security Death Index (SSDI)*

Ancestral Line - Fraternal Side

What follows below was my attempt to trace my lineage as far back as possible using Ancetry.com and FamilySearch.org. Since the goal was to see how far I could go back in, this path crosses both fraternal and maternal bloodlines – whichever path I could find that kept going. There's one obvious weak ink about 400 years back where the male parent was not known, but as we're freely crossing male/female lines, we'll live with it.

The numbers that follow each name is the year of their birth. Keen-eyed readers will note that there are other inaccuracies in the data, such as overlapping times or gaps that cannot be explained in the current records. Consider this "for fun" data and don't make any formal claims to any throne based on it.

Odin (215AD)
Beldeg Odinsson (243)
Brand (271)
Frithoga (299)
Freawine of Saxony (327)
King Wig Freawinesson (355)
Esla Gewisson (411)
Elesa (439)
Cedric of the West Saxons (467)
Cynic of Wessex (525 - bad date)
Coewlin ruler of West Saxons (530)
Cuthwine Wessex (556)
Cutha Wessex (592)
Ceolwald (622)
Cenred (644)

Ingild (680)

Eoppa Atheling King of Wessex King of West Saxons (706)

Eaba of Wessex (732)

Ealhmund Under-Kent (732)

Egbert (784)

Ethelwulf (Aethelwulf) Kind of Wessex (806)

Alfred The Great King of England (848)

Edward the Elder King of England (874)

Edward I, King of England (921)

Edgar the Peaceable of England (943)

Edmund (966)

Edmund II (The Exile) Aetheling (992)

Edmund Prince of England (1016) - married daughter of Conrad II Holy Emperor of Rome (990)

Malcolm III of Scotland (1031)

David I Mac Malcolm (1084)

Henry of Huntingdon (1114)

William The Lion Dunkeld (1143)

Alexander Dunkeld (1198)

Alexander Hoo (1170)

Robert Hoo (1274 - hundred year jump!)

Thomas Hoo (1315)

William Hoo (1342)

Thomas Hoo (1366)

Thomas Lord Hastings Hoo (1396)

Geoffrey Boleyn (1420)

Robert Tilden (1460)

Richard Tilden (1485)

Richard Tilden (1520)

Thomas Tilden (1541)

Nathaniel Tilden (1583)

? / Elizabeth (1603 weak link)

John Sprague I (1630)

John Sprague II (1660)

Benjamin Sprague (1686)

Benjamin Sprague (1725)

John Sprague (1749)

Amasa Sprague (1788)

Milton A Sprague (1832)

Elmer H. Sprague (1863)

Bernard Sprague (1897)

<recent generations omitted>

Odin

Ancestral Line - Maternal Side

This section is included for the benefit of my family and direct ancestral line. It won't be of much help to other Spragues. Maybe you can find a path that crosses this one. I did the same exercise as before but starting with my maternal line. Although, as before, there are some odd dates and spans that can't be fully explained, but it was great fun to discover a path that went as far back as possible... to Adam and Eve. Naturally, inaccuracies are inevitable, but it was still exciting to find this path using the available records, which is as close to official as we can get. Some names are followed by odd values (ex: LJYB-Q56). These are record numbers in the FamilySearch.org database if you want to jump straight to these records.

Adam (4000BC L6R1-3F9)

Seth ben Adam Second Patriarch

Enos (3765BC)

Cainan, son of Enos

Mahalaheel, son of Cainan

Jared, son of Mahalaheel

Enoch (LVC4-81C)

Methuselah

Lamech

Noah

Shem

Arphaxed

Salah

Eber

Peleg

Reu

Serug

Nahor

Terah

Abraham (1800BC-1500BC LJYB-Q56)

Son of Abraham Isaac Terah (1922BC)

Jacob ben Isaac King of Goshen (1892BC)

Joseph (huge time jump)

Marcomir the First King of the Sicamber and Troy (500BC)

Antonor the Second King of the Sicamber and Troy (475BC)

King Priam King of the Sicamber and Dardina (450BC)

Herennlius Lucius valerius of dardina (425BC)

Valerius Laevinius of Dardina (385BC)

Flavius Valerius Constatinius of Dardina council of Rome (360BC)

Constantine the First of Dardina council of Rome and Roman Emperor (335BC LJYL-X3X)

Constantius Appius Sabinus of Dardina (310BC)

Appius Cladius Sabinus of Dardina (285BC)

Appius Cladius of Dardanian (260BC)

Claudius Gothcius of the Dardina (230BC - discrepancy jumped from 225AD to 230BC))

Eutropious Nobleman of Dardanian (225)

Constantius Chlorus I (242)

The Great Emperor Falvius Valerius Constatinius (271 LH26-C81)

Flavius Honorius Theodosius (300)

Flavius Theodosius I (347 age anomoly)

Emperor Honorius of Western Rome (347)

Alaric the Bold Visigoths I (370 anomaly - age with next two)

King Wallia of the Visigoths (Valla) (380)

King Rechila Suevic of Galicia (370)

King Gonthaires Gunderic de Bourgogne (410)

Godogisel de Geneve (450)
Agilulf Agilofing
Teobaldo de Baviera (470)
Garibald I (496)
Carloman de Landen Mayor of the Palace Australia (550)
Pepin Mayor of the Palace (564)
Ansigise Mayor of the Palace (605)
Pepin Mayor of the Palace (635)
Charles "Martel" Mayor of the Palace (676)
Pepin The Short King of the Franks (714)
Emperor Charlemagne (742 MSVH-KG6)
Roi d'Italie Pippijn Karloman Der Franken (773)
Roi Bernard Van Italy (797)
1st Count Pepin Quentin of Vermandois (815)
Heribert I, Count of Vermandois (Count of Senlis) (850)
Duke William I Of Normandy (893)
Richard The Fearless Duke of Normandy I (933)
Robert D'Evereux (964)
Raoul de Beauffou (954)
Richard De Beauffoe (984)
Hugh De Mountfort (996)
Hugh De Montfort (1020)
Stephan De Monyn
Sir Alexander Monyns
Simon Monyns
Robert Monyns
John Monyns
Simon Monyns
Nicholas Monins
John Monins (1392) (age anomoly son at 63?)
John Crafford (1455)
John Crafford II (1479)
John Crayford III (1505) (dupe)

Edward Crayford (1529) (dupe)
William Crafford (1555) (dupe)
Sir Guy Crafford (1430) (anomaly - out of place)
John Warren (1561)
Thomas Warren (1624)
Robert Marriott (1599 LCXR-VWL)
Lawrence Mizell (1614)
James Bynum (1666)
William Bynum Sr (1690)
William Bynum Jr (1720)
Jesse Bynum (1765)
George Bynum (1785)
Caleb H. Gilley (1806)
William Peterson Gilley (1828)
John Caleb Gilley (1848)
William Peterson Gilley (1865)
<recent generations omitted>

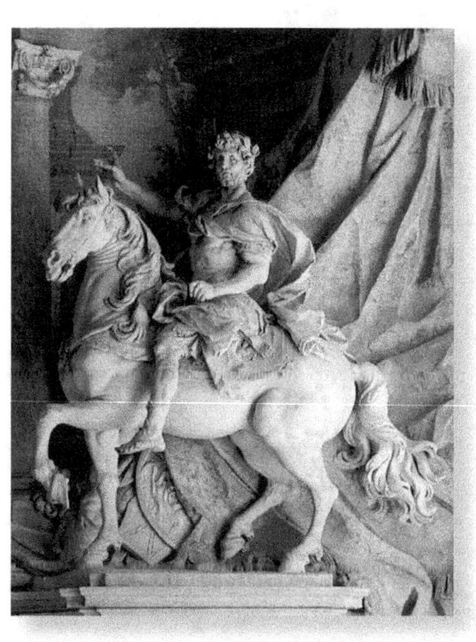

Charlemagne (2 April 742/747/748[1] – 28 January 814), also known as **Charles the Great** or **Charles I**, was King of the Franks. He united most of Western Europe during the early Middle Ages and laid the foundations for modern France and Germany. He took the Frankish throne in 768 and became King of Italy from 774. From 800 he became the first Holy Roman Emperor

Relative Finder. aka BYU Roots

Some clever programmers at Brigham Young University wrote a web app (https://www.relativefinder.org) that uses the FamilySearch.org database to find all paths from you to various famous people. Below is my filtered list

Relative	Relationship	Your Mother-Father Ch	Relative's Mother-Fath	Relative's PID
Henry David Thoreau	5th Cousin 4 times removed	FFFFFFMFFF	MMFFMF	LC5F-1M4
Hiram Ulysses Grant,	5th Cousin 5 times removed	FFFMMMFFMFF	FFMMMF	LZKL-91F
Lucille Desiree Ball	7th Cousin 1 times removed	FFFMMMFFF	MFFFMMFF	L71K-6KZ
Jacob Vernon Hamblin	6th Cousin 4 times removed	FFFMMFMFFMM	FMFMMMM	KWZP-8X6
James Madison	5th Cousin 6 times removed	MMFFMFMMFFFM	FFMMFM	LZTD-MFS
Marion Robert Morrison	8th Cousin	FFFFFFFFF	FMMFMFMMF	LZTB-DMS
William Howard Taft	7th Cousin 2 times removed	FFFFFFMMFM	MMMMMFFM	KPHL-SSM
Franklin Delano Roosevelt	7th Cousin 3 times removed	FFFMMMFFMFF	MFFFFMMF	LHVX-MPP
Warren Gamaliel Harding	8th Cousin 2 times removed	FFFMMMMFFFF	FFFMFFMFF	2B2X-SLL
(Pres.) John Adams	6th Cousin 7 times removed	MMFFMFMMFFFMMF	FFFFFFF	LZKH-L4F
James A Garfield	7th Cousin 5 times removed	FFFMMMMFMFMMF	MMMFFMMF	LZ6W-F3Y
Jesse Woodson James	8th Cousin 3 times removed	MMFFMFMMFMFM	MFFMMFFFM	LHR8-7K6
Millard Fillmore	7th Cousin 5 times removed	FFFMMMMMMFFFF	MMMFMFFF	KTZJ-1Q3
Nathaniel Hawthorne	8th Cousin 3 times removed	FFFMMMMFMFMM	FMMMMMMFM	KGM1-9CS
Theodore Roosevelt	6th Cousin 7 times removed	MMFFFMMFMFMFFF	FMMFFFF	L85X-19L
Truman Osborn Angell	6th Cousin 7 times removed	FFFMMFFFFFMMFF	MFMFMFF	K2QF-MM1
Amelia Mary EARHART	10th Cousin	FFFMMMMMFMM	MFFMMFMFFFM	LCLF-57G
George Washington	7th Cousin 6 times removed	FFFMMMMMMFMFFF	FFMFFFFF	LVCR-WBH
Harry S Truman	9th Cousin 2 times removed	MMFFMFMMFFFM	MMMMMMMMFM	9WST-5VX
Robert Lee Frost	7th Cousin 6 times removed	FFFFFFMFFFMMFM	FMMFMMFM	LHSW-XQP
Buster Keaton	10th Cousin 1 times removed	FFFFFFMFFFMF	MFFFFFMMMFF	LCJ4-3XK
Elvis Aaron Presley	10th Cousin 1 times removed	FFFMMFFFFMFM	FMMMFFMMFFM	L64M-357
Pres. Richard Milhous Nixon	8th Cousin 5 times removed	MMFFFMMFMFMFFF	MMFMMMMFF	LZNG-673
Walter Elias Disney	9th Cousin 3 times removed	FFFFFFFFFFFFF	MFFFFMFFFF	L84S-ZRN
David Stern Crockett	9th Cousin 4 times removed	FFFMMMMMFMFMMF	MFFFFMFMFF	L8SR-ZBH
Gerald Rudolph Ford	9th Cousin 4 times removed	MMFFFMFFFMFMMM	MFMMFFMFMM	L7BZ-71C
Humphrey De Forest Bogart	10th Cousin 2 times removed	FFFMMFFFFMFFF	MFMFMMMMFFF	LZ4K-B6H
Rutherford Birchard Hayes	9th Cousin 4 times removed	FFFFFFMMMFMMMF	MMFMFMFMMF	MMQX-4SH
Susan Brownell Anthony	10th Cousin 2 times removed	FFFMMMFFMFFFF	MMFMMFMMFMF	L7GY-8LD
Barack Obama	12th Cousin	MMFFFMFMFMFMF	MMMFFMMFMMFFF	BARK-OBM
Emily Elizabeth Dickinson	10th Cousin 4 times removed	MMFFMFMMFMFFFFF	FMMMFFFFFFF	LZJW-XR2
Lyndon Baines Johnson	10th Cousin 4 times removed	FFFFFFMFFFMMFMF	FFFMFFFMMMF	2M79-4JT
Benjamin W. Harrison	11th Cousin 3 times removed	FFFFFFMFFFMMFMF	FMMFFMMFFFMF	LZY7-6G9
Henry Jaynes Fonda	11th Cousin 3 times removed	FFFMMFFMMFMMFMF	MFMFFFMMFMFF	KLJY-7XF
John Calvin Coolidge Jr.	11th Cousin 3 times removed	FFFMMFFFFMFMFFM	MFMMMMFFMMFM	L85X-GPZ
Philo Taylor Farnsworth	13th Cousin	FFFMMMMMFMFMMF	FFFFMMMMMMFMFF	KWCQ-PFY
Louis Dearborn L'Amour	13th Cousin 1 times removed	MMFFMFMMFFFMMFF	MFFMFFFMFMFFFF	LZLZ-BQ5
Samuel Langhorne Clemens	14th Cousin	MMFFMFFMFFFFMFM	FFMMMFMMMMFFFMI	LZJ1-TLQ

Final Word

The Internet has changed the world in so many ways, not the least of which is in genealogy research. There's just so much information out there at your fingertips.

As you may have read several times now, I never expected to find much about my family, so it's hard to describe the feeling I got when, in the course of just a couple of hours, I went from thinking I had no pedigree to seeing my place in the human tree. I found where I came from, how we got here, and some great stories and achievements of my ancestors. I hope that this book will give you a jump start - will motivate you to continue your search for your family roots.

There are many web sites dedicated to ancestry, military records, birth and death records. The two I found to be the most useful are **Ancestry.com** and **FamilySearch.org**.

Ancestry.com has the most data - countless images of census records and everything you can imagine to help validate your connections. FamilySearch.org is a close second (and in some ways exceeds Ancestry) and has a great, user-friendly interface. I usually use Family Search for the high-level research, and Ancestry.com for the detailed research.

FamilySearch.org is maintained by *the Church of Jesus Christ of Latter-day Saints* and is offered free with no obligation. The church believes that the family is eternal, the most important thing in the universe, and the primary way in which we can understand God's love for His children. The Family is our primary reason for our time on Earth, which is why the church is committed to helping anyone and everyone learn and appreciate their ancestry.

Some of the larger church meetinghouses even have Family History centers where trained volunteers can help you get started. Go to https://familysearch.org/locations/ to see if there's a family history center near you. Many non-members even plan vacations to Salt Lake City in order to visit the main Family History Center in order to work on their genealogy.

Ancestry.com is a commercial service and you must pay a subscription fee to use it. If you *are* a member of the LDS church and don't already know this, you also get free access to Ancestry.com. Major bonus.

So go on, get out there and start discovering your own family history…

If you a vested interest in all-things-Sprague, and would like to contact me regarding ways to make a future edition more useful, or just to say 'hi', the following email address should be around for a while: wildlizardranch@gmail.com

Fondly,
Jeff

www.ingramcontent.com/pod-product-compliance
Lightning Source LLC
Chambersburg PA
CBHW072025290526
45787CB00015B/1945

9781519361714